THE
FRENCH
PARADOX

THE FRENCH PARADOX

Understanding
Contemporary
France

F. ROY WILLIS

HOOVER INSTITUTION PRESS
Stanford University / Stanford, California

Acknowledgments

Tables 2.2 and 2.4 reprinted with permission of OECD (Organization for Economic Cooperation and Development).
Table 3.3 reprinted with permission of *Politique Etrangère*.
Portions of Table 4.2 reprinted with permission of MIT Press, copyright 1979 by the President and Fellows of Harvard College.

HOOVER PRESS PUBLICATION 264

Library of Congress Cataloging in Publication Data
Willis, F. Roy (Frank Roy), 1930–
 The French paradox.

 Includes bibliographical references and index.
 1. France–Foreign relations–1969– . 2. France–Economic conditions–1945– . 3. France–Armed Forces. I. Title.
DC412.W55   944.083   81-83070
ISBN 0-8179-7642-6   AACR2

Contents

Tables

Introduction

Americans have always recognized the cultural greatness of France, but they are usually a little surprised to be asked to recognize as well the economic and military strength of France and hence its political importance to the United States. French idiosyncracies can be shrugged off, or accepted with bemused tolerance, if one assumes that the aberrant country is a lightweight in world affairs. France, however, is a very important power. Economically, France ranks fifth in the world in gross national product. In Europe, it is second only to West Germany, and it has been closing the gap between them throughout the 1970s. Its GNP in 1972 was $310 billion compared to West Germany's $406 billion—76 percent of its neighbor's GNP. In 1978, the contrast was $376 billion for France compared to West Germany's $468 billion—80 percent of the German product.[1] It has also been steadily catching up with the living standard of the United States. In 1972, the French GNP per capita was $5474 compared to $6876 for the United States. In 1978, while the American GNP per capita had risen to $7783, the French had reached $6876. In short, in only six years, the French had reduced the

American superiority by 23 percent.[2] Moreover, France had become the world's third largest exporter, exceeding even Japan, while at the same time it was making serious efforts, by boosting its nuclear generation capacity, to reduce the burden of oil imports on its balance of payments. In 1980, it was already the world's second largest producer of nuclear power, and it expected to cover 70 percent of its needs in electricity from nuclear plants by 1990.[3] (This plan was, however, cut back because of environmental impact by the Socialist government of President François Mitterrand chosen in 1981.)

Militarily, moreover, France is far from being a minor power. It has possessed the atomic bomb since 1960, and it has deployed a deterrent atomic force comprising nuclear submarines, aircraft, and fixed rocket launchers. It has a well-trained army of half a million people, and imposes a one-year period of conscription on its male population. To handle rapid, short-term intervention, particularly in Africa, it has developed an effective strike force that has been frequently used to maintain (or on occasion to overthrow) regimes in the Third World.

France's determination to follow an independent foreign policy—independent, that is, of the United States and therefore often disconcerting and even repellent to the American administration and public alike—may well have been an advantage to the Western alliance. France has succeeded, albeit at the cost of alienating Israel and Israel's friends in the United States, in keeping close ties with most of the Arab world, including such countries as Iraq with whom American relations have been far from harmonious. It has kept in existence in Africa a francophone community composed of its former colonies and increasingly of Zaïre, a community that has often been a moderating influence in the conflicts of that continent and has contributed to the creation of a multipolar world (as opposed to the bipolar world of the early days of confrontation of the Western and Soviet blocs). France even claims to be able to mediate at times of Soviet-American deadlock, such as that following the Soviet invasion of Afghanistan in 1979, although it has been difficult to see in such actions more than precipitate opportunism ultimately damaging to France's own interests. France, in short, is a powerful state. It is certainly the most difficult of America's allies to understand and the most prickly to handle. It is the basic thrust of the argument of this book, however, that France—no matter how immediately irksome its pretensions to independence of action and how self-righteous its outbursts of nationalism—has been and will remain an extremely valuable partner of the Western alliance in general and of the United States in particular. The evolution of this independent foreign policy since the Second World War is analyzed in Chapter 1. "The Gaullist Legacy" was, in simplest terms, the determination: not to be a junior partner of the United States; to create a European Europe as a counterpoise to the power of the American colossus; to encourage the appearance of a multipolar power structure in the world in place of the bipolar structure of the Cold War; to act as the defender of the interests of the Third World; and, when possible, to use the military and economic power of France in regions like Africa to manipulate events in accordance with the French world view. This legacy has been largely accepted by all French parties except the Communists and will almost certainly continue to influence the policies of Socialist President François Mitterrand. The second chapter documents the economic miracle that has transformed France since the 1950s and that was prerequisite for the assertion of national independence in foreign policy. The French military structure, discussed in Chapter 3, is planned to give to the makers of French foreign policy the means on which international influence is based: deterrence of attack from the Soviet Union by possession of a credible nuclear strike force, capacity to fight a conventional war for the defense of France on its own soil or on the territory of neighboring European countries, and mobile intervention forces, capable of undertaking rapid though small-scale action primarily in the Third World.

The actions France has taken from this base of strength have served the Western alliance in several different ways. In French-speaking Africa, France has contributed generously to the economic development of some of the most poverty-stricken peoples in the world, while attempting to ensure political stability for their governments, where necessary, by direct military intervention. As Chapter 4 shows, this intervention has not always been successful (most notably in Chad), and at times it has been misguided (above all in the support of the sadistic regime of Jean-Bedel Bokassa in the Central African Republic). But the French, acting quite often in spite of vociferous condemnation by some African countries, have undoubtedly been in most cases a needed force for political continuity and responsibility in a volatile area, and by their presence, and indeed by their very independence of action, they have spared the United States both the need to intervene and the opprobrium of having intervened. In the Middle East, in spite of the disastrous bloodletting of the Algerian war, the French have been able to reestablish relatively good relations with almost every power of the region, from conservative Morocco to radical Iraq; only in the past two years have they finally begun to lose hope of keeping the expansionist fervor of Libya's Colonel Gaddafi within bounds by maintenance of amicable relations. The value of France's similar determination to maintain good relations with all the Communist powers (discussed in Chapter 6) is more questionable, although it can be argued that France's support of the particularist views of Poland, Rumania, and especially China has tended to further fragmentation of the Soviet bloc. Probably the most valuable of all France's contributions has been in Europe. Its nuclear force has stood as a symbol of the refusal of Western Europe to accept any bargain that would lead to denuclearization and hence to neutralization or perhaps finlandization. Its military planners have slowly moved toward a renewed coordination of planning with the other NATO powers, while trying, for domestic political reasons, to avoid the appearance of rejoining the military structure of the alliance it left in 1966. The harsh decisions that made the Common Market into something close to an economic union were forced on its partners by France, which also provided in the close Franco-German alliance a powerful but not exclusive reconciliation around which Europe could be formed.

This, then is the French paradox that will be examined in detail in the following pages: that, while pursuing and at times *by* pursuing an independent policy—which was conceived primarily to remove France from the influence of the United States—France has in fact served the interests of the Western alliance and of the United States more effectively than if it had chosen to remain an unassertive and less than enthusiastic partner. As we point out in the concluding chapter, in specific recommendations for the policy that the United States should follow toward France, France behaves as a "model ally" as long as, and only as long as, it is permitted to create what is genuinely a "special relationship" with the United States in the belief that it is achieving the goals of national self-interest.

1

The Gaullist Legacy

Gaullist resentment of the United States has a long history. When General Charles de Gaulle took over the government of France in August 1944, he had already determined that he himself had suffered at American hands a series of humiliations directed at France itself. Perhaps the worst had been his summons to the Casablanca conference in January 1943, following the Anglo-American invasion of Algeria and Morocco, to appear, as he wrote later, "as a prisoner on French soil." His fury at American pretensions represented by President Roosevelt is summarized in a classic passage from his *War Memoirs* that encapsulates his conception of American goals that remained with him when he returned to power in 1958:

> A kind of messianic impulse now swelled the American spirit and oriented it toward vast undertakings. The United States, delighting in her resources, feeling that she no longer had within herself sufficient scope for her energies, wishing to help those who were in misery or bondage the world over, yielded in her turn to that taste for intervention in which the

instinct for domination clothed itself. It was precisely this tendency that President Roosevelt espoused.[1]

Even after the D-Day invasion of France, Roosevelt was reluctant to hand over power to de Gaulle, who was compelled to demonstrate the massive support he was receiving from the Resistance forces before being permitted to take control of France as the American armies advanced toward Germany. Because of this treatment, once de Gaulle had been installed as head of the government in Paris, he determined to win for France its accustomed role among the great powers by the time-honored method of display of military strength. He cast the French army of 500,000 men into southwestern Germany, ignoring the battle plans established by American commanders at the crossing of the Rhine; and he ordered the French First Army to capture Stuttgart before the Americans, in spite of its assignment to the American army. For a brief period it seemed that American troops might end the Second World War as they had begun in November 1942—by fighting French troops rather than German!

Perhaps the most unfortunate and flagrant insult to de Gaulle's pride was the refusal of Roosevelt (and Stalin) to invite him to the Yalta conference in February 1945, where only Churchill's strong advocacy won for France the right to a zone of occupation in Germany and thus a future position of equality in the diplomatic negotiations on Germany. Even more astonishing, given the fact of French participation in the occupation of Germany, was President Truman's assumption that the French ought not to be invited to the Potsdam conference in July 1945. It was hardly surprising that de Gaulle should have threatened after Potsdam to block the implementation in Germany of any decisions with which he did not agree.

In spite of de Gaulle's determination to regain for France a major role in international affairs, up to the time of his precipitate resignation in January 1946 his preoccupation with the internal reconstruction of France had prevented him from laying down a foreign policy greatly at variance with that of the United States—except perhaps for a tendency to seek a special relationship for France with the Soviet Union and for his famous statement that he sought a Europe unified "from the Atlantic to the Urals." A primary reason for de Gaulle's resignation was, in fact, his belief that a strong, independent France could only be created under a powerful presidency and that the bickering political parties had no intention of creating such a position for him to assume.

The constitution of the new Fourth Republic, which was intended to give France a new political start after the discrediting of its institutions by the collaborationist policy of the Vichy regime during the German occupation, was finally ratified at the end of 1946 and was regarded by the American government with restrained satisfaction. The electoral and parliamentary system adopted encouraged the multiplication of parties and prevented the appearance of a strong leader who would assert his ability to disagree with American policy. The Communists were ejected from the government of Socialist Paul Ramadier in May 1947 and were consigned to limbo (or rather to a role of almost totally negative opposition) for the next three decades, even though they represented the fairly constant vote of one-fifth of the electorate. A slightly smaller number of representatives of the Right, most notably the newly formed Gaullist party ("the Rally of the French People"), were usually also excluded. Power was shared throughout the new Fourth Republic by a coalition extending from the Socialists through the moderate Right. Since most of the members of these parties were strongly anti-Communist, they tended to be pro-American.

In addition, circumstances in the late 1940s and early 1950s combined to make French governments dependent upon what de Gaulle called "the Atlantic colossus." In the winter of 1947 emergency aid had to be granted to France to forestall the imminent collapse of the French economy. Marshall aid (which totaled $2.7 billion from 1948 to 1952) was the essential support for the economy's reconstruction and enabled France to achieve a gross national product 45 percent higher than that of 1939 by the end of the Marshall Plan. Although there had been in France considerable opposition to acceptance of Marshall aid once the Soviet Union had refused it, the advances of communization in Eastern Europe combined with the increasingly disruptive strike activity of the Communist trade union ended those hesitations, and a large majority in parliament voted in favor of membership in the Western European Union in 1948 and in the North Atlantic Treaty Organization in 1949. France indeed had become one of the staunchest European supporters of the United States, and almost as a reward, the headquarters of the Marshall aid authorities (now the Organization for Economic Cooperation and Development) and of NATO were located in Paris or nearby.

The United States for its part had become the staunchest supporter of

French efforts to suppress independence movements in their colonies because it had begun to equate colonial independence with Communist expansion (at least in France's colonies if not in most of Britain's). Whereas Roosevelt had often stated that his postwar goal was independence of the colonial possessions of all the European powers, Presidents Truman and Eisenhower channelled massive economic and military aid to the French in their colonial war. In the four years prior to their ouster from Indochina in 1954, the French had received from the United States $2.6 billion for the Indochina war, a sum equivalent to 80 percent of French war expenses.[2] In the case of the long Algerian war, however, the United States proved unsympathetic to French attempts to maintain control, and at the collapse of the French Republic in 1958, the colonial issue had created sharp tension between the two governments without the United States being able to influence French intentions in any significant way. In retrospect, and in particular with the lesson of American involvement in Vietnam in mind, it is doubtful whether increased American aid would have altered the outcome of the French struggle in Vietnam or whether increased pressure could have speeded up the outcome of the Algerian war. The moment for potentially successful intervention had been in 1945 and 1946, before years of bloodshed had created a legacy of distrust and opened fissures within societies that were eventually to gain their independence.

To the United States the most pleasing aspect of the foreign policy of the Fourth Republic was its advocacy of European integration. Throughout the postwar years, the United States supported the strengthening of Western Europe by a closer integration of the national economies, with the ultimate goal of the creation of a United States of Europe. Marshall's offer of aid in 1947 had been based on the assumption that the European powers would harmonize their economic policies to avoid waste of American resources, but the American government was disappointed to find that once aid was forthcoming the European recipients had rapidly reverted to virtually independent national planning. Hence, when, on May 9, 1950, French Foreign Minister Robert Schuman proposed the creation of a European Coal and Steel Community (ECSC) open to all countries of Western Europe, in which coal and steel (as well as the labor and capital of the coal and steel industries) would circulate freely, his speech was hailed by the American administration as a major step forward. Even the French proposal to create a European Defense Community within which a rearmed Germany could participate was supported by the American government, until the plan was rejected in 1954 by the French themselves. Above all, the creation of the European Economic Community (EEC), or Common Market, in 1958 was seen to offer the best potential for the economic and political strengthening of Europe.[3]

Thus, in spite of the near-chaos of French political life at the end of the Fourth Republic and the animosity caused by the Algerian war, the foreign policy of the governments of that Republic was in large measure in harmony with that of the United States. The return of de Gaulle to power in June 1958 abruptly changed this cooperative arrangement.

De Gaulle was welcomed back to power in France (and his return was at first greeted with relief by the American government) because he appeared to be the only person who could end the political indecision, avoid a coup d'état by the French army in Algeria, and solve the Algerian problem. During the first four years (1958-1962), in which he wrestled with the Algerian question and with the problems of reviving the French economy, relations with the United States were relatively calm. His decision in 1960 to permit the French colonies in Africa to opt for independence was regarded as an act of far-sighted statesmanship, especially as it was followed by the peaceful and generally amicable creation in Black Africa of a number of new states that remained tied by economic and cultural links to France, and hence to the Western alliance. From the moment that Algerian independence was recognized in 1962, however, de Gaulle unveiled a wide ranging program of foreign policy that was in many ways in direct contrast with that of the United States and was in some specific ways directed against the United States.

De Gaulle frequently satirized "the somewhat elementary conviction which animates the American people concerning the primordial mission which ought to fall to the United States, as if by a decree from Providence, and the preponderant role which falls to them by right."[4] Yet he had no doubt of the mission, destiny, and moral duty of France to play a major and independent role in world affairs. In his *Memoirs of Hope* he described his concept of that role: "The same destiny which permitted us during the terrible crisis of the [Second World] war to achieve the salvation of our country now offered it, in spite of everything which it had lost in relative strength and riches in the past two centuries, an international role of primary importance, suited to its special genius, corresponding to its self-interest, and in proportion with its means."[5] The world in which the new French government would operate was threatened, in de Gaulle's view, by its division into alliance systems subordinate to the two major powers that would inevitably end in the fearsome confrontation of atomic war. In spite of his frequent condemnation of the Communist system, he persisted in portraying the United States and the Soviet Union in a similar light, because only then could he justify the independent role he wished France to follow. "The two empires," he wrote, "the American and the Soviet, which had become colossi in relation to their former strength, were opposing their forces, their spheres of influence, and their ideologies."[6] In this situation it was essential for France to become itself a new pole of world power, detaching itself gradually from its obligations to the American alliance system and thus precipitating the disintegration of the American bloc from within. But at the same time France was to encourage a similar break-up of the Soviet bloc. Thus de Gaulle's withdrawal of France from military participation in NATO in 1966 went hand in hand with his wooing of the Rumanian government and his recognition in 1964 of the Communist government of China. He hoped to see disintegration of the Communist bloc while maintaining good relations with all its members, including the Soviet Union itself. Characterizing his policy as "détente, entente, et coopération," he sought improved relations with Eastern Europe at least ten years before West Germany adopted a similar policy under the label of *Ostpolitik*.

De Gaulle's second sphere of action was in Western Europe, whose states would, he hoped, follow the French example and pull slowly away from their subordination to the United States in order to form a "European Europe." The foundation for such a Europe was to be Franco-German understanding. His conditions for good relations with Germany were outlined to Chancellor Adenauer at their first meeting in September 1958: German acceptance of the borders established in 1945 (and thus recognition of the German loss of the Oder-Neisse territories), renunciation of atomic weapons, patience with regard to a future reunification of Germany, and a genuine attempt to seek an understanding with the Communist regimes of Eastern Europe. If West Germany had accepted those conditions, de Gaulle was prepared to make Franco-German alliance the keystone of his European policy, and he might well have attempted to use the Franco-German Treaty of 1962 to create such an alliance if the German *Bundestag* had not written in so pro-American a preamble as to destroy its value to de Gaulle. De Gaulle was still prepared to settle for "organized cooperation," however, especially as closer ties with West Germany would have proved disturbing to the other members of the Common Market with whom he intended to establish a second level of intimacy within his European Europe. As conceived by the politicians of the Fourth Republic, the European Coal and Steel Community and the Common Market were, de Gaulle believed, little more than mechanisms for perpetuating American domination in Western Europe. The organizations were marked by their bureaucratic character, dominated by countryless (*apatrides*) technocrats moved by a moralistic urge to dissolve the nations of Europe within a supranational union run by them. The pretensions of these Eurocrats reached their most intolerable heights when Walter Hallstein was president of the EEC Commission, and for that reason, de Gaulle blocked his reappointment in 1967.

De Gaulle's underlying fear was that the ultimate goal of the advocates of supranationalism was to destroy the nations that were the greatness of Europe. As he remarked in one of his most famous press conferences: "Dante, Goethe, Chateaubriand, belong to all Europe to the very extent that they are, respectively and eminently, Italian, German, and French. They would not have served Europe if they had been countryless, or if they had thought and written in some integrated 'Esperanto' or 'Volapük.'" Worst of all, the disappearance of Europe's nation-states would leave the new European Community as no more than an "American protectorate," while the admission into the Community of new members, especially Britain which he felt to be an American Trojan horse, would convert it into "a colossal Atlantic community dependent upon and controlled by the United States, which would soon have absorbed the community of Europe."[7]

One vitally important sphere of action for de Gaulle's France was to be in the Third World. "We have given up domination," he claimed, "and are trying to promote international cooperation. . . . France alone can play this role, France alone is playing it."[8] He displayed constant, almost paternalistic solicitude for the economic suffering of the poorer countries of the world and set the example for other countries by donating in aid a larger percentage of the French gross national product per capita than that of any other country in the world. But, as always, he linked this action to strictly political goals, namely, the maintenance of French influence among its former colonies.

Finally, to ensure respect for France's world ambitions he determined to restore the economic and military strength of France itself. A strengthened presidency and a disciplined parliament were to ensure that France would speak with one voice in world councils. A resurgent economy encouraged by a stable currency and a governmental policy of expansionism were to provide the means by which the new foreign policy could be waged successfully. Above all, no matter what the cost of its development, France was to possess its own atom bomb and its own means of launching it—a *force de frappe*.

The new constitution was written and approved and an expansionist economic policy implemented during the next six months, from June to December 1958, during which he governed in the absence of a parliament. Close ties were established with West Germany and a personal friendship developed with Konrad Adenauer. The Common Market was made responsive to French economic interests by the threat on several occasions of the use of veto power to ensure that by 1962 an agricultural policy of great benefit to France was implemented parallel with a policy of industrial integration. Britain's application for membership in the Common Market was vetoed in January 1963, and the European Commission's pretentions to supranational power were squelched in 1966–1967 by withdrawal of French representatives from the operation of the Community for a period of seven months. Closer relations with Russia were established by frequent summit conferences and were maintained by a deliberate attempt to play down the significance of the Soviet invasion of Czechoslovakia in 1968. Possible dissidents within the Communist bloc received visits of state by de Gaulle such as that to Rumania in 1968. Above all, de Gaulle slowly broke French ties with the United States. Convinced that the rough parity in atomic strength of the Soviet Union and the United States would lead them to conduct any military confrontation in Western and Eastern Europe instead of launching rockets against each other, de Gaulle determined that France must withdraw from the American military bloc. Even before the successful explosion of the first French atom bomb in 1960, he had withdrawn the French fleet from NATO and had banned the introduction of American atom bombs and creation of launching pads on French soil. In 1966 he took the ultimate step of withdrawing all French forces from NATO and compelling the transfer of NATO headquarters from France to Brussels.

De Gaulle's foreign policy was popular with every politically active group of the French population with the exception of the more convinced supporters of European integration who never forgave him for his attacks on supranationalism in Europe. By 1969 almost all segments of the French population from the Communists to the extreme Right approved the goals of French independence from American leadership (especially at the time of American involvement in Vietnam), possession of a military force powerful enough to deter any eventual aggressor, manipulation of the Common Market to safeguard French interests, and development of a multipolar world.

Following the election of Georges Pompidou as president in 1969, little major change in the principles of Gaullist foreign policy was expected. Pompidou himself had been a loyal Gaullist since his first days of collaboration with the general in Algeria during the Second World War. He had served faithfully as de Gaulle's premier from 1962 to 1968; and it has even been suggested that his dismissal by de Gaulle in 1968 as a kind of scapegoat for the May riots might have been de Gaulle's subtle way of preparing him for the presidency—by disassociating him from the general's own unpopularity. Gaullist votes had given Pompidou a solid victory in the presidential election, and he appointed reliable Gaullists as premier: Jacques Chaban-Delmas from 1969 to 1972 and Pierre Messmer from 1972 to 1974; and in Michel Jobert, his truculent foreign minister from 1973 to 1974, Pompidou had one of the most uncompromising defenders of the Gaullist line. In the aftermath of the Soviet invasion of Czechoslovakia, however, world circumstances were unsuitable for any rousing reassertion of Gaullist aims in the spectacular way that de Gaulle had favored. Regular summit meetings continued to be held with the Soviet Union, but little was achieved. Nuclear weapons production was scaled down for reasons of economy, and new weapons systems were postponed. France remained isolated from the significant negotiations on arms limitation between the blocs—from the SALT I talks between the United States and the Soviet Union and from the Mutual and Balanced Force Reduction (MBFR) talks between NATO and the Warsaw Pact powers. Pompidou at first opposed the Helsinki Security Conference, even though such a conference was directly in line with de Gaulle's European policy; but, after persuading the European

Community to establish common principles in the talks, Pompidou became far less distrustful.

Pompidou was less certain than de Gaulle of either the value or the solidity of the Franco-German alliance. As West German Chancellor Willy Brandt pressed ahead with negotiation of new relations with the Soviet Union and with the countries of Eastern Europe, and in particular as Brandt established working, if not amicable, relations with East Germany, Pompidou became obsessed with the notion that Germany might settle for neutralization as the price paid for reunification, and let President Nixon know that he was in favor of maintenance of American troops in Germany. His fear of a neutralized Germany was in part the cause of his opposition to the MBFR talks.[9] Worry about Germany too may well have pushed Pompidou to his major break with Gaullist policy —the decision to permit British membership in the Common Market. He had declared as early as 1968 that, if elected president, he would bring Britain into the Community; and from 1970 to 1972, during the negotiations on British entry, the French delegates, although bargaining strongly for France's self-interest in the accession agreement, worked effectively to achieve an agreement the British government could accept. Pompidou even attempted to use the enlargement of the Community — with the admission in 1973 of Britain, Denmark, and Ireland—to stimulate political support for his presidency.

By calling for a referendum on admission of the new members in 1972, Pompidou hoped to demonstrate vast electoral support for all aspects of his foreign policy; but while 36 percent of the electorate voted in favor, about 40 percent stayed home. The vote did demonstrate what many critics have emphasized about French foreign policy—that it had been kept secret from the people for so long as one of the prerogatives of a centralized state that the French public had simply lost interest and turned to more pressing problems such as inflation and unemployment.[10] Pompidou's more understanding attitude toward Britain did not lead to an improvement of relations with the United States. Secretary of State Kissinger and Foreign Minister Jobert in particular seemed to have an instinctive animosity, and Jobert quickly squelched Nixon and Kissinger's notion in 1973 of holding a summit meeting with the European governments for the purpose of signing a new Atlantic Charter.

Pompidou's most successful advance from de Gaulle's positions lay in developing French presence in the Mediterranean and Middle East.

This policy was directly displeasing to the United States government because it involved first a further lessening of France's support for Israel and a strengthening of ties with Israel's avowed enemies, especially with Libya and Iraq. In January 1969 de Gaulle had placed an embargo on the shipment of 50 Mirage Jets to Israel, even though they were largely paid for; Pompidou agreed in 1970 to sell 110 Mirage planes to Libya. During the 1970s arms exports, particularly to the Arab countries, became a major part of French commerce.[11] When the economic crisis precipitated by the Arab-Israeli War of 1973, the temporary oil embargo by the Arabs, and the quintupling of prices by the Organization of Oil Exporting Countries (OPEC) struck, France was able to declare that it was relying on a strategy of direct relations with individual Arab suppliers rather than on a concerted effort by the West under American leadership to compel better conditions from the oil suppliers. In the Washington conference of February 1974, Jobert was at his most intransigent in blocking American efforts to persuade the oil importing countries to form a common front toward OPEC.

For France as for all the Western countries, the oil crisis precipitated an economic recession that was to last throughout the 1970s and into the 1980s, a recession that compelled a reassessment of France's foreign relations and thus a reexamination of the legacy of de Gaulle in foreign affairs. This reassessment was carried out by the new president, Valéry Giscard d'Estaing, after Pompidou's sudden death of cancer in April 1974.

In 1980, looking back over the first six years of the presidency of Valéry Giscard d'Estaing, Raymond Aron declared: "Giscard d'Estaing is following a foreign policy which in its essentials does not differ from that of Georges Pompidou or of General de Gaulle, even though the international context has changed."[12] More novelty had in fact been expected of this young (forty-eight years old) president who had declared in his first press conference, "I am a conservative who likes change." Although Giscard had been elected with Gaullist support (but with a majority over Socialist challenger François Mitterrand of only 50.81 percent of the vote), he was not a member of the Gaullist party, but of a small moderate-conservative group called the Independent Republicans. Moreover, in his first Cabinet, which was headed by Gaullist Jacques Chirac, he included the Democratic Center party leader Jean Lecanuet and Radical leader Jean-Jacques Servan-Schreiber as well as a number of nonpoliticians. Moreover, all his foreign ministers—Jean Sauvagnargues (1974–1976), Louis de Guiringaud (1976–1979), and Jean François-Poncet (1979–1981)—were career diplomats and not politicians. Yet the essential lines of Gaullist policy were retained and in some cases even reinforced. Giscard was an even more enthusiastic supporter of détente than de Gaulle (and perhaps even than Brezhnev), and in 1980 he was considerably criticized in France itself for the unseemly haste with which he traveled to Poland to meet with Brezhnev after the Russian invasion of Afghanistan. Like de Gaulle, too, he felt that French influence (which he called "*rayonnement*") must be extended throughout the Third World. In the Middle East he used the French provision of arms and nuclear technology to reinforce ties with the Arab states and to help cover the cost of oil imports, which was becoming increasingly burdensome throughout his presidency. In Africa, France interfered militarily on several occasions—most notably in Chad, in Zaïre, and in Mauritania. Giscard's personal extension of this essentially Gaullist policy was his call for a north-south dialogue that was to be followed by the granting of vastly increased economic aid by the industrialized world of the north to the underdeveloped world of the south.

Relations with the United States remained poor. He displayed only a mild tolerance for President Gerald Ford and an openly critical impatience of President Jimmy Carter. For this reason, and because of immediate personal empathy with West German Chancellor Helmut Schmidt who took office at almost the same time as Giscard, the Franco-German alliance became closer than at any time since the retirement of Adenauer. With Schmidt even more openly contemptuous of Carter than Giscard, the two governments made it evident that they saw Western Europe becoming increasingly responsible for its own fate as the American economy crumbled, its political direction vacillated, and its military became demoralized. The much debated defense policy that Giscard implemented in 1976 was far from being a break with Gaullist policy, which the more intransigent members of the Gaullist party suggested. Its two basic changes—the reinforcement of conventional arms and the extension from France itself to all Western Europe of the area of so-called sanctuarization within which the French nuclear umbrella would be extended—were readjustments of the French defense role in Western Europe primarily for the benefit of West Germany.

The one genuine novelty of Giscard's policy, his support for the election of the European Parliament by universal suffrage in 1979, strength-ened the European Community in a way that de Gaulle might well have disapproved. Yet the strengthening of the European Community, particularly by French cooperation with West Germany, was un-doubtedly an extension of the Gaullist view that a European Europe must be strong enough to act alone. As Giscard told the magazine *L'Express* in May 1980:

> Facing the Soviet Union, which is maintaining its policy line, the West has become weak. It is disorganized, in the sense that it no longer has a line of action which is clearly understood by those who are questioning themselves about it, in particular by the Third World. The problem is first of all that of the West. Often they say to us: "It's your fault, you French, you don't maintain close enough ties with the United States." I do not believe it. On the contrary, it is extremely important that there should exist in the world a European personality; and that European per-sonality presupposes that countries like France should affirm their ability to act or to decide.[13]

Foreign policy disagreements played only a small part in the presiden-tial election campaign of 1981, in which the Socialist party leader François Mitterrand defeated Giscard d'Estaing on the second round of balloting by the surprisingly large majority of 51.7 percent. As the leader who, after 1971, had brought new life to the moribund Socialist party, Mitterrand had turned increasingly to internal issues, and espe-cially to the alienation of the half of the French population that had felt largely unrepresented since the return of de Gaulle to power in 1958. The central themes of his campaign therefore tended to be France's economic and social problems, for which his solutions included nation-alization of the remaining private banks and of eleven industrial com-panies, creation of 1.6 million jobs by reducing the work week to 35 hours and by state employment, and increasing other social benefits. His concern for the state of the French economy promised certain inter-national repercussions. Within the European Community, greater pro-tection of French interests was to be expected, while some restriction of the flow of Japanese imports was also possible. International companies operating in France could expect to find the increase in government par-ticipation in the economy more threatening to their activity. The crucial fact was, however, that the election had not been a plebiscite on the Gaullist legacy in foreign policy. Giscard d'Estaing lost for a number of reasons that were unconnected with his foreign policy. Unemployment had reached 1.7 million; inflation was over 13 percent; and the majority of the French felt that the economic policies of his premier, Raymond Barre, had failed. Giscard d'Estaing's aloof personality and his increasingly authoritarian attitudes had disenchanted many of his former supporters, and scandal had stained his image as a leader of impeccable character. Infighting between the two parties of the Right—his own Union for French Democracy and the neo-Gaullist Rally for the Republic (RPR)—had led many in the RPR to abandon Giscard on the second round of voting. Perhaps most important was the fact that the prospect of fourteen years under the same president was more than many voters could endure. In short, Mitterrand was elected for economic and social change and for the new style of leadership that he had promised.

In foreign policy the prospect appeared to be one of gradual change within the Gaullist legacy, remodeling it to relate to the enduring concerns that had been the finer aspects of the policy of the Fourth Republic, as the decisions taken during Mitterrand's first months in office showed. His foreign minister, Claude Cheysson, was a professional diplomat who had served for eight years as a member of the Commission of the European Community, and Cheysson immediately set out to emphasize the commitment of the new government to strengthened Atlantic ties and to a reinforcement of the European Community. Both he and Mitterrand took a strong line with reference to the Soviet Union, condemning the Soviet involvement in Afghanistan and condemning the imposition of martial law in Poland. At the same time, they expressed concern at the buildup of Soviet SS-20 missiles in Eastern Europe and implied that they favored the deployment of American Pershing-II missiles and cruise missiles with NATO forces in Europe as a counterbalance to Soviet strength. The French president also reaffirmed his long-standing support for Israel, although he made clear during a state visit to Israel in 1982 that he favored creation of a Palestinian state.[14] He had previously strongly condemned the Israeli destruction of the French-built nuclear reactor in Iraq. In relations with the Third World, Mitterrand, too, seemed to be modifying rather than completely reworking the principles of Gaullist policy. French economic aid to the Third World was to be increased by 25 percent, a sign that the new government viewed aid to economic development as a higher priority than political or military intervention. Indeed, Mitterrand caused considerable surprise in France by seeking better relations with the government of Chad President Goukouni Oueddi, the protégé of Libyan President Mouammar Gaddafi, and he canceled all aid to Goukouni's rival Hissène Habré whom Giscard d'Estaing had supported. He even restored the supply of military equipment to Libya, which had been canceled by Giscard d'Estaing after Gaddafi's forces had intervened in the Chad civil war on behalf of Goukouni. Nevertheless, Mitterrand's renewal of ties with such old personal friends as Ivory Coast President Félix Houphouet-Boigny was a signal to French-speaking African states that the carefully nourished friendship of the past two decades remained of great importance to France. With few exceptions, therefore, the foreign policy of Mitterrand gave promise of being even more compatible with that of the United States than the policy of de Gaulle, Pompidou, and Giscard d'Estaing—somewhat against the intentions of its authors—had become.

2

The Economic Basis
of French Independence

No one knew better than de Gaulle that a policy of national independence must be based upon economic strength. "Politics and economics are tied one to the other as action is to life. . . . What [a country] is worth in the physical sense of the term and, consequently, the weight it carries in its relations with others, form the basis on which of necessity are founded the strength, the influence, the greatness, as well as the relative degree of well being and security which for a people, on this Earth, it has been agreed to call happiness."[1] As Jean Fourastié has recently pointed out in his book *The Thirty Glorious Years or The Invisible Revolution*, between 1946 and 1975 France experienced an economic miracle of a kind never before seen in French history.[2] It was this economic miracle that made possible the Gaullist break with the foreign policy of the Fourth Republic. For that reason the character of this economic transformation must be looked at in some detail before we turn to examine the impact of the oil crisis on the French economy after 1975.

The most important fact is that the real national income per capita tripled, while the population, which had been stagnant since the late nineteenth century, rose from 40 million in 1946 to 53 million in 1975. (Indeed, the population growth stimulated one of de Gaulle's greatest flights of fantasy when he looked joyfully and inaccurately forward to a population of 100 million Frenchmen by the end of the century.) By 1975, France had achieved a gross national product of $338 billion compared with an American GNP of $1541 billion or a French GNP per capita of $6423 compared with an American $7148.[3] France had in fact achieved the tenth highest standard of living in the world.[4]

Structurally, changes in the agricultural sector had been greatest. The number of people working in agriculture had fallen from 7.4 million in 1946 to only 2 million in 1975—from 36 percent of the working population to only 10 percent.[5] This rural exodus was both the cause and the result of a successful restructuring of agricultural production. The flight of many from the land, combined with governmental measures of financial support, had enabled large, efficient farms to be created from millions of fragmented holdings, particularly in the rich agricultural lands of the Paris Basin and the north. The availability of capital through such banks as Crédit Agricole and from government funds enabled a technological revolution to be implemented in the countryside. In the famous tractor craze of the 1950s, the number of tractors rose to 625,000 (from 37,000 in 1945). A similar increase took place in the use of chemical fertilizer and in the use of improved seed and livestock.[6] The result was a rise in productivity, not only per farm worker but also per acre. The national average production of wheat tripled, of corn quintupled, and of grapes and potatoes more than doubled. With large agricultural surpluses available—particularly of cereals, meat, and dairy products—agriculture was able to play a major role in the French balance of payments. For example, in 1974 when France ran a deficit of 34 billion francs in foreign trade, agricultural exports counted for a positive balance of 5.9 billion.[7] At the same time, however, the pressure of the farming population on the government to dispose of their surplus at prices guaranteeing a decent standard of living required de Gaulle and his successors to put constant pressure on their Common Market partners to create the Community's common agricultural policy (CAP) and to guarantee the establishment of agricultural markets for French products within the Community at prices frequently above world levels. As we shall see in considering France's role in the European Community, French pressure to maintain the financial burdens of CAP remains one of the greatest sources of discord within the European Community and one of its greatest ongoing problems. At the same time it should be remembered that the improvement in agricultural productivity has been shared unequally by the French regions. Vast areas of the south and southwest remain agriculturally backward, so that the contrast between the rich and poor agricultural areas of France remains one of the deepest internal rifts within French society.

The real miracle of the French economy was not, however, in the agricultural sector but in the industrial. Taking 1938 as base year (100), French industrial production had, as a result of the war, fallen to a level of 84 by 1946; but by 1974 it had reached an index of 499.[8] These figures imply a total restructuring of French industry during this thirty-year period. Certain of France's older industries became stagnant or entered deep depression, particularly the industries most vulnerable to competition from the Third World or from Japan. The coal mines of the north, for instance, after making an important contribution in the immediate postwar period, went into a sharp decline in the mid-1950s. Steel, which did soar longer due to the stimulus of the European Coal and Steel Community, also began to decline in the mid-1960s, throwing Lorraine into depression. Mass-produced textiles, particularly in Lorraine and Alsace, felt the hot winds of Asian competition in the mid-1970s. Shipbuilding, particularly because of Japanese competition, was in almost constant crisis. Among the more traditional industries, only food processing remained strong, particularly in its contribution to French exports. The building industry and government construction soared in importance, almost doubling its work force between 1946 and 1975 as a result of the extraordinary work of reequipment that was carried through in France during this period. Construction of railroads and métros, or subways, made France the world's expert in transportation systems by 1970. During the 1970s, France's exports of transportation equipment exceeded the total of its next three competitors, and the French constructed subway systems throughout the world, including such countries as Mexico and Venezuela.[9] Perhaps the most impressive achievement from the point of view of the average French person was housing construction. France had constructed only 350,000 lodgings between 1935 and 1939. Between 1968 and 1975 it constructed 4 million. In 1975, 35 percent of French homes (not including vacation homes) had been constructed since 1949, although the legacy of nine-teenth-century building was still evident in the fact that 26 percent of French houses still did not have an indoor toilet.[10] France, moreover, had pushed its way into the forefront of advanced technology. As we shall see in detail later, the French arms industry, which by 1980 was employing 300,000 people, was one of the outstanding examples of this advance, with products varying from the Mirage jet fighters of the Dassault Company to missiles from Matra and machine gun carriers from Panhard. The French were in the forefront of Europe for the pro-duction of rockets both for military and peaceful uses and had become so proficient that they could sell to American Telephone and Telegraph Company, against the competition of American producers. Automobile production was so efficient that by the 1970s Renault had exceeded both Volkswagen and Fiat in European sales, and both Renault and Peugeot were mounting a concerted attack upon the American market. The total number of private automobiles in France had risen from 1 mil-lion in 1946 to 15.5 million in 1975.[11] The French chemical industry, headed by giants like the Rhône-Poulenc Company, was in many ways ahead of the American. In plastics, the French had developed a whole line of products, from the cooking utensils of Moulinex to the ball point pens of Bic, that played a not insignificant role in French exports. Mov-ing from their hold on the high-priced luxury market in such products as clothes and perfume, French companies entered the mass market both in France and abroad with skis and all types of name brand merchandise.

Many factors explain this industrial expansion. Governmental eco-nomic policy has been largely beneficial. The five-year (later four-year) plans have been "indicative," meaning that they laid down the direc-tions in which the economy was expected to move and in which govern-mental investment would be made, without attempting to direct indus-try in the character of its investment. Nationalized firms have in general been well run, as the example of Renault shows; and governmental in-vestments in infrastructure, while frequently criticized for their tardi-ness, have given France the necessary underpinnings for a modern in-dustrial system. Educational investments have been extremely effective in raising the quality both of the management of industry and of the work force. The international economic situation was also helpful until 1974. The rise of the West German economy undoubtedly stimulated the French, and as early as the 1950s West Germany became France's principal trading partner for both exports and imports. The foundation of the ECSC and of the Common Market provided French firms with a duty-free trading area in which they rapidly increased their exports. The labor force was constantly replenished, due to the high birthrate, the migration from agriculture, and immigration—of French citizens from the newly independent colonies, of workers from the Common Market, and of unskilled labor from the countries of the Mediterranean Basin. Although France's trade unions made frequent use of the strike weapon for both political and economic ends, the situation rarely reached the level of paralysis that affected the British economy. Perhaps most important of all, as can be seen from the type of companies that advanced most rapidly in the French industrial sector, a new generation of management cast away the traditional Malthusianism of French business— the determination to avoid risk, the desire to retain a stable rather than an expanding market, the refusal to innovate—that characterized French industry in the prewar years. For example, Michelin's early experiments with the radial tire gave it its hold on the world market for tires.

The tertiary sector was also larger and healthier than at any previous period. Employment in this sector had advanced from 32 percent of the working population in 1946 to 51.4 percent in 1975, with the principal increase occurring between the censuses of 1968 and 1975, that is, when the industrial transformation was already well advanced.[12] Commerce and services had doubled their employment. Wholesale and retail commerce had by 1975 a total employment of 2.2 million and displayed an extremely healthy shift to a more efficient large-scale marketing system from the preponderance of small, inefficient, family-run shops that for more than a century had been one of the greatest sources of weakness in the French distribution system. Just over 3 million were employed in other services of the kind increasingly demanded by the consumer society that France was becoming—in garages, hotels, ski resorts, and the like. Also important for the expansion of the economy was the great increase in support of education by the government. By 1975 France had over 12 million pupils in preschool, elementary, and secondary schools and over 1 million students at the university.[13] These figures do not merely represent an increase in the number of French youths due to the high birthrate of the postwar years; they also indicate a revolution in

French education. Preschools had become so widely extended by 1970 that 90 percent of children aged four and 67 percent of children aged three were attending preschool. In 1967 the age of children leaving school had been raised to sixteen. With 54 percent of its fifteen- to eighteen-year-olds attending school in 1970, France had far exceeded the level of Great Britain (39.4 percent) and of West Germany (30.5 percent), while remaining well behind the United States (82.9 percent). Finally there had been an impressive upgrading of French higher education with a highly desirable, if still inadequate, shift away from law and the humanities toward science and technology. Education and culture accounted for 25 percent of the French budget, compared with 17.5 percent for defense, and were by far the largest item in state expenditure.[14]

Thus, from the end of the Second World War to 1975, France had carried through an extraordinary economic transformation. The fact that it had achieved an annual growth rate of 5 percent, whereas in all its previous history it had never achieved more than 2 percent, was at the basis of the new confidence in French ability to play an independent and ambitious role in world affairs. The world economic crisis that began with the quintupling of oil prices in 1974 (to approximately $10 a barrel) and was worsened by the second petroleum crisis of 1979–1980 (when prices rose to about $32 a barrel) was to test whether French economic independence could continue. During its thirty-year expansion, France had become increasingly dependent on oil as its principal source of energy. Whereas in 1955 oil provided one quarter of French energy supplies, in 1973 it provided two thirds. France had covered 65 percent of its own energy needs in 1955, but in 1973 it covered only 24 percent, and in 1976, in spite of efforts to cut down oil consumption, only 20 percent.[15] France had become the third largest importer of oil in the world, after Japan and the United States, its principal suppliers being Saudi Arabia, Iraq, and Iran (Table 2.1). France, however, had also seen a great drop in its coal production, which fell from 54 million tons in 1965 to 25 million tons in 1976, causing an increase in importation of coal from 17 million tons in 1965 to 22 million tons in 1976. What was even more remarkable, however, was the fact that France was a net importer of meat, fruit and vegetables, textiles, shoes, and chemicals; and in the case of many other products, such as business machines and many types of light engineering goods, it was barely able to maintain a balance between its exports and imports. The French balance of trade since 1973 has thus been consistently unfavorable (Table 2.2), and seemed likely to worsen following the brutal doubling of oil prices in 1979.

To reduce this imbalance the French sought first to increase sales to the oil producers themselves, and did succeed in increasing exports of capital goods and machine tools and of some types of military equipment. In 1975–1976 alone, the French did succeed, through increased exports, in reducing by a billion francs their deficit with the oil producing countries, but the effort soon flagged. A second area in which increased exports were sought was with the Soviet Union and the Communist countries of Eastern Europe, but here again the burden of excessive debt that those countries assumed forced them to cut back on Western imports by 1978. Clearly France's main hope for increased sales lay with its partners in the Common Market and in the United States. The Common Market countries accepted 50.4 percent of French exports and the United States 5.14 percent in 1977. There were already clear signs in the late 1970s that French exports to the Common Market were beginning to flag, and French desire to postpone entry into the community of such countries as Spain and Greece, whose agricultural products might compete with the French, was obviously for protection of its most important market.

TABLE 2.1

SOURCES OF FRENCH OIL SUPPLIES, 1978

Country	French Imports (millions of dollars)
Saudi Arabia	3820
Iraq	1974
Iran	1126
Nigeria	868
Abu Dhabi	719
Algeria	663

SOURCE: INSEE, *Tableaux de l'économie française, 1980* (Paris: INSEE, 1980), p. 141. Figures have been converted from francs to U.S. dollars at the exchange rate of 4.83 francs equal to U.S. $1.

NOTE: Oil was also purchased from Venezuela, Libya, and the Gulf Emirates. Figures include total trade, primarily in oil products.

TABLE 2.2

FRENCH BALANCE OF TRADE, 1973–1979

(Millions of Dollars)

	Exports (fob)	Imports (cif)	Balance of Trade
1973	35,948	37,380	− 1,432
1974	45,896	52,819	− 6,923
1975	52,211	54,241	− 2,030
1976	55,812	64,390	− 8,578
1977	63,514	70,493	− 6,979
1978	76,467	81,678	− 5,211
1979	97,981	106,874	− 8,893

SOURCE: OECD, Etudes économiques, France (Paris: OECD, May 1980), p. 79.

For the United States, French economic difficulties are a source of immediate concern, just as American economic problems are a cause of
worry to the French. In the first place, the United States has consistently run a favorable balance of trade with France and would like to
keep on doing so. As Table 2.4 shows, in 1978 French exports to the
United States totaled $4.27 billion, while American exports to France
were $5.78 billion. Trade with the United States thus accounted for
$1.51 billion out of a total French deficit in foreign trade of $5.21
billion. Agriculture comprised about one quarter of American exports.
Within the industrial sector, the principal exports were aircraft, office
machinery, electrical machinery, and scientific equipment. As long as
French sales to America were luxury goods such as perfumes, high-
fashion apparel, and wines, there was little concerted criticism of French
competition by American business circles. In the 1970s, however, while
France maintained such traditional exports as alcoholic beverages,
French industrial companies began to penetrate the American market.
Exports of rubber tires to the United States, principally from Michelin,
reached $180 million; automobile sales exceeded one-third of a billion
dollars; and iron and steel exports were over half a billion dollars in
value. Clearly, increases of French exports in these areas of the economy
would be of great concern to the troubled American tire companies,
automobile manufacturers, and iron and steel producers. Weaker American companies were even welcoming French investment in their opera-

TABLE 2.3

FRENCH FOREIGN TRADE, 1977

(Millions of Francs)

Country	FRENCH IMPORTS			Country	FRENCH EXPORTS		
	Rank	Quantity	Percentage of Total		Rank	Quantity	Percentage of Total
West Germany	1	64,057	18.49	West Germany	1	53,334	17.09
Italy	2	33,148	9.57	Italy	2	32,679	10.47
Belgium-Luxembourg	3	31,121	8.99	Belgium-Luxembourg	3	31,093	9.96
United States	4	24,042	6.94	Great Britain	4	20,295	6.50
Saudi Arabia	5	21,173	6.11	United States	5	16,046	5.14
Netherlands	6	21,142	6.10	Netherlands	6	15,943	5.11
Great Britain	7	18,085	5.22	Switzerland	7	12,215	3.91
Spain	8	9,682	2.80	Algeria	8	8,824	2.83
Iraq	9	8,979	2.59	Spain	9	8,148	2.61
Switzerland	10	7,892	2.28	USSR	10	7,349	2.35
Japan	11	6,795	1.96	Morocco	11	4,749	1.52
Sweden	12	5,738	1.66	Nigeria	12	3,681	1.18
USSR	13	5,680	1.64	Sweden	13	3,617	1.16
Iran	14	5,416	1.56	Norway	14	3,427	1.10
Abu Dhabi	15	4,904	1.42	Iran	15	3,348	1.07
Benin	16	4,638	1.34	Ivory Coast	16	3,259	1.04

Algeria	17	3,875	1.12	Saudi Arabia	17	3,034	0.97
Ivory Coast	18	3,782	1.09	Austria	18	2,984	0.96
Brazil	19	3,425	0.99	Tunisia	19	2,637	0.84
Canada	20	2,626	0.76	Canada	20	2,562	0.82
Total (all countries)		346,207	100.00	Total (all countries)		311,550	100.00

Source: Edgard Pisani et al., *La France dans le conflit économique mondial* (Paris: Hachette, 1979), p. 54.

tions on the home market. Peugeot, which had already bought up Chrysler's Simca subsidiary in Europe, loaned $100 million to the faltering parent company in the United States in 1979. Renault saw collaboration with American Motors as its chance to increase its sales outlets in the United States and envisaged future production of a Renault car in American Motors's factories.[16]

In the second place, American companies in France were deeply involved in the health of the French economy through direct financial investment. In 1975, American companies held a majority interest (20 percent or more of the shares) in companies employing 275,000 people with total sales of $20 billion—that is, in companies with 6 percent of French industrial employment, 10 percent of industrial sales, and 8.3 percent of the year's industrial investment. Moreover, American companies in France held a minority interest in companies employing a further 307,000 people with sales of $22 billion. The weight of American involvement was thus enormously important, especially in such companies as business machinery, oil, agricultural machinery, and chemistry; and weakness in those sectors of the French economy would have had immediate repercussions on several of the American multinational corporations.[17] Moreover, certain of these investments, notably the American stranglehold on French business machinery and information processing by such companies as IBM, had already been under attack during de Gaulle's presidency, and it was to be expected that further weakening of the French balance of payments would bring increased pressure to restore such important segments of the economy to French national control. A veritable outburst of anger at American power within the French economy had broken out in France in the 1960s. (This was a decade of very rapid growth of direct American investment, which reached $2.59 billion in 1970.[18]) De Gaulle had even launched a *Plan Calcul* intended to free the French business machine industry of American influence. Yet all of France's principal efforts at independence failed during the 1970s. Although a French reactor for nuclear power was created at great expense, it was finally decided that it was cheaper to buy American designs and American uranium and to abandon the French invention. The principal French computer company, formed by the union of several smaller companies under the auspices of the government, was allowed to fuse with American-owned Honeywell-Bull in 1975, although the French company did retain a 53 percent control of the new enterprise.[19] American technical knowledge and capital, as creators of employment in France, were not likely to be rejected in the new fervor of nationalist self-assertion.

In the third place, the United States is concerned that France will search for greater trade with Russia and its satellites in Eastern Europe, even at the expense of having to seek an accommodation with such Russian military aggression as that in Afghanistan in 1979. When President Carter decided in 1980 to put pressure on Russia by reducing American trade—cutting the delivery of cereals by 17 million tons and banning new sales of goods of strategic interest or high technology—the French foreign minister announced that the French had "no intention of modifying [their] commercial relations with the Soviet Union."[20] These relations had in fact been improving rapidly since the meeting of Giscard d'Estaing and Brezhnev in June 1977 at the Château of Rambouillet. The tripling of Franco-Soviet trade planned at that meeting had been achieved by 1979; and in 1979 the French were rewarded for acceptance of the Soviet views on détente and peaceful coexistence by large contracts for several French firms. In particular, Péchiney Ugine-Kuhlmann, the French aluminum firm, was to build a large factory in Siberia under a contract worth $750 million. The new computer company (C.I.I.—Honeywell-Bull) picked up a $20 million contract that President Carter had compelled Sperry Univac to cancel.[21] In short, France had become dependent to some degree upon Russia for the trade surplus of $250 million, and some firms were virtually reliant upon the Soviet Union for their continuing prosperity.[22] The Soviet Union was the principal foreign client of the steel group, Creusot-Loire, which supplied it with special steels, heavy engineering products, and even complete factories. Between 1974 and 1978 it received orders totaling $1.5 billion. Ten thousand of the twenty thousand employees in the machine tool industry were working on supplies for Russia. Maintenance of these good economic relations was certainly a factor in persuading Giscard d'Estaing to keep open relations with Russia in spite of the Afghan invasion, condemning the invasion verbally but taking no concrete steps that would injure French economic interests in the Soviet Union.

In the fourth place, the United States is affected by increasing French competition for sales to the oil producing countries, whose capacity to absorb Western goods appeared severely limited in relation to the vast

TABLE 2.4

Structure of Franco-American Trade, 1978

Categories of Goods Traded	American Exports to France (millions of dollars)		French Exports to U.S.A. (millions of dollars)	
	Total	Selected Subcategories	Total	Selected Subcategories
Food and Live Animals for Food	637	Meats 126 Cereals 264 Fruit 82	146	
Beverages and Tobacco	13		339	Alcoholic Beverages 316
Raw Materials	566	Oilseeds 248 Pulp and Waste Paper 74	87	
Mineral Fuels	198	Coal 95 Petroleum 95	104	Petroleum 87
Animal and Vegetable Oils	31		0	
Chemicals	517		697	Inorganic Chemicals 385 Perfumes 50

Manufactured Goods	521			1147
	Paper Products	66	Rubber Tires	180
	Textiles	134	Glassware	40
	Iron and Steel	23	Iron and Steel	553
Machinery and Transportation Equipment	2431			1195
	Office Machines	555	Office Machines	119
	Electrical Machinery	446	Road Vehicles	365
	Aircraft	792	Aircraft	154
Miscellaneous Manufactures	858			550
	Scientific Equipment	267	Apparel	138
			Works of Art	27
Miscellaneous	4			7
Total	5776			4272

Source: OECD, *Statistics of Foreign Trade. Annual: Tables by Reporting Countries 2/1978, Series B.* (Paris: OECD, 1979), pp. 58–77.

reserves of foreign currency those countries were accumulating. In no sphere was this competition among Western exporters, and especially between France and the United States, more politically delicate than in the matter of arms sales. French arms sales increased eightfold between 1970 and 1980, making France the world's third largest arms exporter, after the United States and the Soviet Union. According to the United States Arms Control and Disarmament Agency, in the five years before the oil crisis (1968–1972), French arms exports in current dollars were $1.48 billion or $2.1 billion in constant (1976) dollars. In the five years following the crisis (1973–1977), they increased to $4.45 billion in current dollars or $4.74 billion in constant (1976) dollars. From 1973 to 1977, France's principal clients for arms other than NATO members, were Iraq ($240 million in current dollars), Saudi Arabia ($230 million), United Arab Emirates ($220 million), Libya ($210 million), Pakistan ($210 million), and Morocco ($210 million), while South Africa purchased $450 million worth of arms in spite of the French decision to end arms sales after 1975.[23]

Ironically enough, the French armaments industry was recreated after the Second World War with significant financial aid from the United States. By 1968, France had received over $4 billion in American military assistance, an amount that was four times as much as Great Britain had received.[24] During France's war in Indochina, the United States was paying one quarter of the French defense budget and one half the cost of the French rearmament program. Although this financial aid was intended to help France prepare its forces for the fighting in Indochina and for service in NATO, the French armaments industry began very quickly to search out foreign markets. The lead was taken by the Dassault company, which produced its first jet aircraft (the M.D. Ouragan 450) for the French air force in 1947, and at once sold 60 planes to Israel and 104 to India. Dassault's Mystère fighter produced in the mid-1950s was sold to the U.S. Air Force (225), to Israel (60), and to India (110). Israel at that period was also the principal purchaser of French tanks. During de Gaulle's presidency, French arms sales abroad were regarded as an instrument of foreign policy because they enabled France to become an alternate supplier to countries seeking to avoid dependence upon the two superpowers. At the same time, while a large proportion of the French military budget was being funneled into the development and production of atomic weapons, arms sales helped subsidize both research and larger scale production of conventional weapons. Sales to Israel continued in the 1960s until a partial embargo was imposed after the Six Day War in 1967 and a total embargo was imposed after the Israeli use of French helicopters to attack Beirut airport in 1968.[25] The shift from supplying Israel to supplying Arab countries began almost immediately with the sale from 1971 through 1974 of 110 Mirage fighters to Libya for $400 million.[26] Some of these fighters were reputedly loaned to Egypt for use against Israel in the Yom Kippur war in 1973. Rather than censure Libya for this violation of their ban on re-export of French military equipment, the French decided to lift their embargo on sales to the Mid-East in general. The greatest sales achievement of the 1970s was the contract with Saudi Arabia in 1974 for about $1 billion worth of aircraft, missiles, and armored fighting vehicles.[27]

As Edward Kolodziej has pointed out, by this policy of arms sales France has in fact made itself dependent upon foreign countries for maintenance of its vital arms industry, a curious result in view of the original purpose of the policy, which was to increase French independence. Several of France's most important companies are dependent on foreign clients for an important part of their sales – this is especially true of the Dassault-Bréguet airplane company, Aérospatiale (helicopters, missiles), Société Nationale d'Etudes de Construction de Moteurs d'Aviation (engines), and Thomson-Brandt (military electronics equipment). In all, over 300,000 people are employed in the armaments industry, and over one third of them work on exports.[28] The French government, which acts as the principal sales office for French arms through the Délégation Ministérielle pour l'Armement, is well aware that the United States offers the principal competition in its battle for foreign markets. The famous competition for the "deal of the century" – to supply NATO with over 600 light fighter planes in the late 1970s – fought unsuccessfully by Dassault (which was backed by the French government) against General Dynamics and the American administration, was a lesson in point.[29] And the backing of the trade unions, Communist and non-Communist alike, has been given to the pursuit of such employment-creating sales.

The structure of the French export trade is illustrated by Table 2.5, which notes the export volume of the leading French companies in 1977. As can be seen, five of the principal exporters are automobile producers and a tire producer. Four are heavily involved in arms sales. At

TABLE 2.5

Leading French Exporters, 1977

Exports of More Than Five Billion Francs ($1.02 billion)

1. Régie Nationale des Usines Renault (automobiles)
2. Peugeot (automobiles)
3. Air France

Exports of Three to Five Billion Francs ($0.61 to $1.02 billion)

4. Dassault-Bréguet (airplanes)
5. Citroën (automobiles)
6. Chrysler France (automobiles)
7. Thomson-C.S.F. (electrical equipment)
8. Chargeurs Réunis (transport)
9. IBM France (business machinery)
10. Michelin (tires)

Exports of Two to Three Billion Francs ($0.41 to $0.61 billion)

11. Aérospatiale (airplanes, missiles)
12. Rhône-Poulenc (chemicals)
13. Creusot-Loire (iron and steel)
14. Usinor (iron and steel)
15. Dumez (public works)
16. Alsthom Atlantique (public works)
17. Daval
18. Vallourec (metal pipes)

Exports of One to Two Billion Francs ($0.20 to $0.41 billion)

19. Technip (heavy engineering)
20. Spie Batignolles (public works)
21. SCOA
22. Fives Cail Babcock
23. Berliet (automobiles)
24. Ugine-Kuhlmann (chemicals)
25. Charbonnages de France (chemicals division)
26. Entrepose GTM (marine oil engineering)
27. Aluminum Péchiney (aluminum)
28. SNECMA (engines)
29. Compagnie Générale Maritime (sea transport)
30. Compagnie Française de Raffinage (oil refining)

Source: Pisani et al., *La France dans le conflit économique mondial*, pp. 60–61.

least three are dependent upon the Soviet Union for many of their export orders. The structure of exports of industrial products and of services is thus inadequately diverse, particularly because automobile and arms sales are open to considerable fluctuation and because the Soviet and East European markets can dry up rapidly with a change in governmental economic policy.

Yet in general the achievements of the French economy in the period since the Second World War must not be underrated. The transformation of agriculture has been revolutionary. The industrial sector has known greater progress than at any previous period in French history. The advance of the service sector has modernized the whole social structure of the country.

3

French Military Strength
and National Defense

Since 1968 France has maintained military forces of about 575,000 men, a considerable reduction from the total of 1.1 million at the height of the Algerian War in 1957 (Table 3.1). Approximately 47 percent of these forces are conscripts who serve for one year, the length of service having been reduced from eighteen months in 1970. Since about 300,000 young men become eligible each year, the military forces are unable to enlist all who are eligible and frequently have to change the health requirements in order to incorporate the exact number needed. The majority of the conscripts serve in the army; but most are able to choose the exact date when they are called to service, and half are able to pick the area in which they will serve. Since the other 53 percent of the military forces are professional soldiers recruited on a voluntary basis, France has, regardless of the protestations of politicians to the contrary, the basis of the professional army that General de Gaulle called for in a book he wrote in the 1930s, called *L'Armée de métier*.

These military forces cost 3.7 percent of the gross national income, a total slightly higher than that of West Germany (3.6 percent) but considerably less than those of either Great Britain (5.1 percent) or the United States (6.0 percent), both of which have completely volunteer armies. The French military forces received (in 1978) about 17 percent of the national budget, considerably less than the budget for education and culture which was 25.2 percent. It is particularly interesting to note that French nuclear forces, which in 1978 had only 24,000 men or 4.2 percent of the total military forces, received 17 percent of the military budget and almost one third of the amount provided for military equipment.[1]

A new organization of the armed forces was conceived in 1960 and slowly implemented until the late 1970s. During that period, the armed forces were divided into (1) the Forces for the Operational Defense of the Territory (*Forces de Défense Opérationelle du Territoire*, DOT), (2) the Maneuver Forces (*Forces de Manoeuvre*), and (3) the Strategic Nuclear Forces (*Forces Nucléaires Stratégiques*, FNS).[2]

TABLE 3.1

FRENCH MILITARY FORCES, 1914–1979

(Thousands)

	Land	Sea	Air	Gendarmerie	Total
1914					979
1938	665	77	56	49	847
1949	455	55	66	58	634
1957	829	86	175	63	1153
1962	721	79	140	69	1008
1968	330	69	108	68	575
1975	332	68	102	74	576*
1976	331	68	102	75	576*
1977	330	68	101	76	575*
1978	324	68	101	76	569*
1979	320	68	101	77	566*

SOURCE: INSEE, *Tableaux de l'économie française, 1980*, p. 155.
* Not including forces common to all branches.

The forces of DOT were conceived to be a strictly home-based defense force whose purpose was to hold back the enemy on the frontier, and if necessary, fight a rear guard action as the enemy advanced through the national territory and establish a national resistance following initial defeats. It was to consist of the *gendarmerie* (a national military police normally under civilian control), twenty-one infantry regiments of 750 men each, and four armored car regiments. In times of emergency they were to work closely with the urban police, the riot police (*Compagnies Républicaines de Sécurité*, CRS), and the two intelligence services of the Ministry of the Interior—the political intelligence branch (*Renseignements Généraux*, RG) and the counterespionage branch (*Surveillance du Territoire*, ST). Finally, if mobilization were decreed, these forces were to be joined by a reserve regiment in each of the ninety-six departments. A large proportion of the conscripts was expected eventually to serve in the DOT; the conscripts would thus, in theory at least, have the sensa-

TABLE 3.2

French Defense Expenditures, 1979
(Millions of Francs)

Programs	Operations	Equipment	Total
Strategic Nuclear Forces	1,978	10,290	12,268
Tactical Nuclear Arms	510	1,234	1,744
Classical Forces	23,523	16,423	39,946
Forces in Overseas Possessions	2,007	367	2,374
Research and Development	1,152	1,940	3,092
Advanced Training Programs	4,922	1,816	6,738
Personnel Support	4,270	343	4,613
Equipment Support	2,814	556	3,370
General Administration	2,590	376	2,966
Total	43,766	33,345	77,111
Miscellaneous (Pensions, civilian, military)	15,129		15,129
Total Budget	58,895	33,345	92,240

Source: INSEE, *Tableaux de l'économie française, 1980*, p. 155.

tion of defending their own homes. DOT was never popular with the professional soldiers, who doubted its efficacy, and was suspect as the continuance of forces created in 1947–1948 when internal unrest among the French population seemed likely to result in widespread anti-government violence.[3]

In 1977, the *Forces de Manoeuvre* were composed of two divisions stationed in Germany with headquarters at Baden-Oos and three divisions stationed in France with headquarters at Nancy in Lorraine. Their equipment was planned to reach 148 AMX-30 (main battle tanks) and 36 AMX-13 (infantry fighting vehicles) per division. The divisions in France were equipped with tactical nuclear arms (consisting of Pluto missiles fired from a mobile platform) that remained under the direct control of the French president. Since these missiles had a range of only seventy-five miles, they were regarded as permitting a graduated response to an enemy invader without immediate resort to the full power of the French nuclear system. (If, however, the weapon remained stationed only on French territory, it posed the immediate problem that it could only be used against targets within friendly European countries, which considerably diminished its deterrent value.[4]) The Tactical Air Force, equipped with Mirage III, Mystère IV, and F100 planes, formed part of the *Forces de Manoeuvre*.

Also included in the *Forces de Manoeuvre* were the *Forces d'Intervention* which were intended for rapid deployment outside France, principally in Africa. Pierre Messmer, when minister of the armies in 1962, described them as "always prepared, capable of strategic mobility by air or by sea, and trained to fight on terrain very different from the European theater."[5] They consisted of one parachute division based at Pau in southwestern France, an amphibious brigade stationed at Brest on the west coast of Brittany, and an Alpine division of troops trained for mountain combat, composed of the well-known Chasseurs Alpins. In addition, in 1978, there were 1000 troops in Senegal, 400 in the Ivory Coast, 450 in Gabon, and 1500 in Chad, as well as about 19,000 members of the three services stationed in four commands in French overseas possessions (Tahiti, Réunion, Martinique, and New Caledonia).[6]

In 1977, the French army undertook a major restructuring of its forces. The territorial forces (DOT) were combined with the *Forces de Manoeuvre* to form one integrated body of military forces. The command structure was simplified. New methods of training, including audiovisual and simulation methods of instruction, were introduced. The organizational units within the army were standardized. For example, a tank division was to consist of two tank battalions, two mechanized infantry battalions, one field artillery battalion, one engineer battalion, and one headquarters support battalion. Communication, transportation, and medical and ordnance support were to be concentrated at the division's headquarters. The division was to provide for reconnaissance and security missions through a troop of scouts, while it was also to carry out antitank activity by use of forward area combat vehicles armed with missiles having a range of 4000 meters. In time of peace, the land forces were to consist of five active divisions in addition to the three units maintained for external intervention (the 9th Marine Division in Brest, the 11th Airborne Division in Pau, and the 27th Alpine Division in Grenoble). In time of war, a new mobilization plan provided for expansion of the army to fourteen divisions, ten of which would be formed from the active divisions. Draftees, after serving with one of the active divisions, would be assigned to a reserve unit attached to one of the divisions, so that in time of mobilization that division could immediately incorporate trained reservists.[7]

In addition to its forces attached to the *Forces d'Intervention* and to the FNS, the French navy possessed (1978 figures) 2 conventional aircraft carriers, 1 nuclear and 1 conventional cruiser, 20 destroyers, 29 frigates, and 23 nonnuclear submarines.[8]

When General de Gaulle returned to power in 1958, the Strategic Nuclear Forces were made the supreme component of the French defense system. The first French atomic bomb, developed by the governments of the Fourth Republic, was successfully exploded in the Sahara Desert on February 13, 1960, and had the power of sixty to seventy kilotons of TNT.[9] The immediate problem then posed was to determine the best method of launching the bomb. The decision was taken that the first generation of the *force de frappe* (an expression invented in 1956 by General Paul Gérardot) would consist of Mirage IV bombers that would play a similar role to that of the B-52s of the American Strategic Air Command. The force was to consist of 58 bombers, of which 36 to 38 were to be permanently operational. These bombers would each carry a nuclear weapon of 80 kilotons and would be capable of flying several thousand miles, with fuel supplied in flight. In 1963, the government decided to create a ground-to-ground strategic ballistic missile system to provide an interim deterrent while a launching system from nuclear submarines could be prepared. By 1975 eighteen missile launchers were installed in silos at the Plateau d'Albion in Haute-Provence; each was capable of launching a load of 150 kilotons a distance of 3000 kilometers, i.e., capable of reaching western Russia from France itself. The first French nuclear submarine, the Redoutable, came into operation in 1967 and began regular service in 1971. It was armed with 16 missiles carrying a total load of 500 kilotons. The Sea-to-Ground Strategic Missile (MSBS) had a range of 200–2500 kilometers, with a probable margin of error of less than three kilometers from its target.[10] By 1980, France had five nuclear submarines in service.

This evolution of French nuclear striking power since the opening of the Strategic Arms Limitation Talks (SALT) in 1969 has led the Soviet Union to demand that France be considered within the Western nuclear capability, even though France has steadfastly refused to participate in the SALT talks (see Table 3.3).

TABLE 3.3

EVOLUTION OF FRENCH STRATEGIC NUCLEAR FORCES SINCE 1969

Year	Stage of SALT Talks	Evolution of the French Nuclear Force
1969	Opening of SALT I	36 Mirage IV Bombers
1972	Signature of SALT I	36 Mirage IV Bombers
		18 SSBS (Plateau d'Albion)[a]
		1 SNLE[b] (16 MSBS)[c]
1974	Vladivostok Summit	36 Mirage IV Bombers
		18 SSBS
		3 SNLE (48 MSBS)
1979	Signature of SALT II	36 Mirage IV Bombers
		18 SSBS
		4 SNLE (64 MSBS)

SOURCE: Pierre Lellouche, "La France, les SALT et la sécurité de l'Europe," *Politique Etrangère*, Vol. 44, No. 2 (1979), p. 253.
[a] Ground-to-Ground Strategic Ballistic Missiles.
[b] Nuclear Submarine.
[c] Sea-to-Ground Strategic Ballistic Missiles.

From 1979 to 1981, the modernization plans for both nuclear and conventional forces authorized in the Military Equipment Program of 1977–1982 were upgraded to take into account new estimates of the Soviet capacity to destroy both the land-based silos and the operational bomber and submarine forces of the 1980s, and an attempt was made to prepare for a new generation of nuclear weapons in the 1990s. The modernization of the land-based missiles on the Plateau d'Albion was to be completed in 1981–1982 with the conversion of the original S-2 rockets (each of which fired one warhead of 150 kilotons over a range of 3000 kilometers) into S-3 rockets (which fire one warhead of one megaton over a range of 3400 kilometers). Nine missiles had already been modernized by May 1980. The remainder were expected to be converted by 1982. Although silo protection was being increased, French estimates showed that the increased threat of the Soviet mobile SS-20 Intermediate Range Ballistic Missiles had drastically reduced the possibility that the silos would survive a Soviet attack, and experimentation had begun with an SX mobile system, in which miniaturized warheads tested successfully in the Pacific would be carried in missiles on heavy trucks. Regardless of whether the SX system was adopted, the modernized silos were expected to be retained for at least fifteen years.

A fifth nuclear submarine was put into operation in May 1980, and at the same time a sixth was authorized for operational use in 1985. The sixth submarine, L'Inflexible, was to be equipped with M-4 missiles with multiple reentry capacity and a range of 4000 kilometers. Similar missiles were to be installed in the other five submarines at a rate of one every eighteen months. By 1990, the megatonnage capacity of the Strategic Oceanic Force (FOST) was to be increased by 1.6 times and the number of warheads by 2.6 times and would become even greater if two additional nuclear submarines were constructed, as envisaged by President Mitterrand.

Because the Mirage IVA bombers were regarded as the most rapidly aging component of the French atomic deterrence, they were to be phased out by 1985, although fifteen were likely to be kept for reconnaissance or tactical support. These fifteen would be armed with an improved thermonuclear warhead.

Finally, for tactical nuclear weapons, the Pluto missile was to be replaced with a Hades missile that would increase the range from 120 kilometers to 200–250 kilometers. The neutron bomb, which had been favored by Giscard's party (the UDR), had been opposed by François Mitterrand and the Socialist party; and it seemed possible after Mitterrand's election as president in 1981 that the bomb would not be manufactured.

Whether these nuclear forces, which had cost France 220 billion francs by 1980, had given the country an independent method of dissuasion of an aggressor against the national territory of France is open to considerable doubt. The Mirage bombers lack the sophistication of the most recent Russian and American planes and are vulnerable to attack from a wide variety of Soviet defensive weapons. The small number of land-based missiles in silos on the Plateau d'Albion are also vulnerable to attack by large Soviet missiles, and in fact are sometimes regarded as a provocation to an eventual aggressor to engage in a preemptive strike. The greatest hope for survival of any retaliatory force in the case of a preemptive strike against France lies with the submarine. It has been calculated that, if two submarines survived such an attack, they would be able to launch a sufficient number of missiles against less well defended targets in the Soviet Union—particularly against industrial or urban agglomerations in European Russia—to represent an unacceptable risk to the Soviet Union. Installation of longer-range missiles will increase the area of Russia brought under danger, as will the equipment of the submarines with multiple reentry vehicles.[11]

Yet the relative power of the Soviet and French nuclear threat remained the essential problem for French strategists. Even if the French could inflict heavy damage upon a Russian target (and even that seems increasingly doubtful), the Soviet Union possesses the capacity to destroy the majority of the French population. In spite of all professions to the contrary, therefore, it has remained an essential condition of the evolution of French military strategy that French forces should be viewed in relation to the forces of France's allies within Europe, and however regrettable to Gaullist or Communist thinking, in relation to the forces and strategy of the United States.

The first phase of France's postwar military strategy, that of the Fourth Republic through 1958, was based on the assumption that the United States possessed overwhelming atomic superiority over the Soviet Union and that, in the event of a conflict within Europe, the United States would be prepared to take the risk of atomic conflict with the Soviet Union on behalf of a European ally. In such circumstances it was logical for France to be a member of NATO and to harmonize the deployment and possible use of its forces in Europe within the framework of NATO and under American leadership. The governments of the Fourth Republic determined to develop an independent nuclear capacity primarily to ensure that their wishes within NATO would carry greater weight, while the weapon itself was considered more as a strategic force permitting a long-distance attack than as the basis of an essentially psychological threat, a weapon of dissuasion intended never to be used.

By 1958, however, de Gaulle was convinced that the parity established between American and Russian nuclear forces had made NATO, or at least French reliance upon the American threat of massive retaliation against Russia, outdated. "From the moment when the Soviets acquired what was necessary to exterminate America, just as America had the means to destroy Russia, could one really think that the two rivals would ever come to strike at each other, except in a last resort? But what would stop them from launching their bombs in between the two of them, that is to say, on Central and Western Europe? For the West Europeans, NATO has thus ceased to guarantee their existence."[12] In fact, while de Gaulle was working on the assumption that America would never risk its own total destruction on behalf of Europe, American military strategy was being changed from one of massive retaliation to one of graduated response—a strategy adapted to the defense of Europe in relation to Russia's new nuclear strength. Hence, as proposed by General Maxwell Taylor in 1956–1957 and implemented by President Kennedy in 1961, the American forces in NATO were progressively equipped with a wider range of weapons permitting a more flexible response to pressure than the full-scale unleashing of nuclear war. At the same time, however, the United States was pressing to prevent the proliferation of nuclear weapons, and the French development of a nuclear force was strongly opposed by the American government, in particular by Kennedy. It was therefore not surprising that General de Gaulle's first proposal in September 1958 for the establishment of a kind of nuclear triumvirate within NATO (consisting of the United States, Britain, and France) should have been rejected by both the American and British governments. With this offer rejected, de Gaulle began, piecemeal, to withdraw French forces from the military structure of NATO—a process that was completed in 1966—and to build up the national force of dissuasion. Curiously enough, what de Gaulle had done was adopt for France the doctrine of massive reprisal that was being revised within NATO largely for the benefit of the European states, and he had done it for precisely the reasons he had accused the United States of following – namely, to make France (and not its allies) a sanctuary defended by the use of nuclear weapons. A further ambiguity lay in the French attitude to the defense of Germany. Not only did the French continue to maintain their troops in their barracks in Germany, although no longer as part of NATO, but they made it clear that they also wished to see this region, which was essential for the defense of France itself, protected by American troops. And although they stated, on principle, that it was essential for France to retain its own nuclear deterrent in order to avoid being dragged into a conflict caused by American action in defense of Germany, they opposed the Mutual and Balanced Force Reduction (MBFR) talks for fear that they would lead to a reduction of the NATO forces that would defend France in West Germany.[13]

Since the resignation of General de Gaulle there has been a marked shift in French strategic thinking toward the position of the United States.[14] To disarm his opponents in the Gaullist party, Giscard d'Estaing declared in 1975, "I have reflected for a long time on this problem [of security], and I have come to the conclusion which was that of General de Gaulle and which is that France must have at its disposition an independent defense. France is part of an alliance but she must assure herself of her defense in an independent way."[15] In fact, however, Giscard and his head of the General Staff, General Méry, were shifting French defense priorities. Their first decision was to adopt a doctrine of "enlarged sanctuary" – to include Western Europe and specifically West Germany within the French defense perimeter. In a somewhat veiled way, cooperation with NATO became closer and American approval of the value of the French nuclear forces to the defense of the West was openly sought and won in the Ottawa Declaration of June 1974.

From the point of view of the United States, the present situation has a number of clear advantages. First, it seems certain that France, in its attempt to create an independent and classical army, has spent more money (perhaps more than necessary) and maintained larger forces than might have been the case if it had relied more upon the American nuclear umbrella and the presence of American forces in Europe. It is also possible that, if they had remained fully in NATO, the French would have followed the British and American example and abolished conscription, especially as the draft is both unpopular in France and criticized for its lack of efficacy by a number of military leaders. Second, as the perception of a declining Western strength (specifically of declining American strength) in relation to the Soviet bloc has become widespread in France, it has become more evident that France will, in time of crisis, coordinate its forces with those of NATO and that in fact the preliminary steps for such coordination are under way. Third, it is possible that the existence of a nuclear dissuasion by France will have precisely the effect upon Soviet thinking that General de Gaulle had intended, namely that, if the Soviet Union should become convinced that the United States would not defend Europe with nuclear weapons for fear of a massive destruction on American territory, it would still be deterred from an attack on Western Europe by the possibility of a nuclear attack—even though on a much smaller scale than that which might be mounted by the United States—from the French strategic nuclear forces. Fourth, the possession by France of a relatively effective striking force for use in small-scale operations such as that in Zaïre in 1978 makes it possible for the United States to withdraw from responsibility for at least some parts of the Third World (see Chapter 4). At any rate, it is clear after two decades of relations with a Gaullist or semi-Gaullist France that the United States will gain nothing by attempting to pressure France into fuller participation in the Atlantic Alliance. American leadership has been suspect in France, at least since the Vietnam War and the Watergate revelations, and the increasing economic, and possibly military, weaknesses of the United States in the late 1970s did not win back French confidence. Paradoxically, the very lack of confidence in the United States is what is bringing France back into closer relations with the Atlantic Alliance.

France and
Sub-Saharan Africa

In two areas of the world above all – in sub-Saharan Africa and in the Moslem states of the Mediterranean and the Middle East – France believes it can exercise an independent role of power and influence commensurate with its economic and military strength, perhaps even greater than that justified by its capacity relative to the two world superpowers.

When one looks back at the tragic way France conducted its process of decolonization, it seems extraordinary that the French should be able to claim with any plausibility that they have retained any possibility of influencing those regions. No European colonial power withdrew from its colonial possessions in the period following the Second World War with greater expenditure of resources and squandering of human lives than France. As early as 1945, the British had intervened in Syria to put an end to savage fighting that had broken out between French troops and the Syrians in spite of the recognition by the Free French of the independence of the two mandated territories of Lebanon and Syria.[1] A rebellion in Madagascar in 1947 and 1948 was put down with extreme brutality by the French authorities. Although the official death toll was 90,000, it is certain that thousands more Malagasy died of hunger and in internment camps.[2] In the imbroglio in Indochina, the French lost 91,000 men; the Indochinese lost uncounted numbers more. In the last four years of fighting in Indochina (1950–1954) the French spent more than $5 billion. The Suez invasion of 1956, while unsuccessful in its political goal of overthrowing the regime of Colonel Nasser, seemed to prove that the French had learned nothing from their defeat in southeast Asia, and were determined to transfer their search for old-style hegemony to the Arab world. During the fighting in Algeria, which lasted from 1954 to 1962, the French built up their forces to over a million. When peace finally was negotiated by General de Gaulle in 1962, over 100,000 Moslem insurgents and 10,000 French troops were dead, as well as large numbers of civilians from both the French and Arab communities. Moreover, the methods of the French army in Indochina and in Algeria, faced with guerrilla forces committed to the techniques of revolutionary war, became increasingly inhuman and included torture, illegal arrest, taking of hostages, relocation of whole villages, and possible murder of prisoners.[3]

Once again, it was General de Gaulle who succeeded in transforming France from the position of pariah in the Third World to that of welcome partner. In the process, amazingly enough, he made himself the most popular person in Africa.[4] In a sense, Pierre Mendès-France had prepared the way for the new policy by negotiating in relatively friendly circumstances the independence of Morocco and Tunisia, which was achieved in 1956. Those two countries, Morocco under a conservative monarchy and Tunisia under the popular nationalist leader Habib Bourguiba, had retained close economic and cultural ties with France. De Gaulle went infinitely further than Mendès-France. The new constitution of the Fifth Republic, written after de Gaulle's return to power in June 1958, had attempted to assuage colonial grievances by grant of greater internal autonomy to the colonies and by the explicit guarantee of the right to independence. A negative vote on the constitution by the people of any of the colonies (except Algeria), de Gaulle announced, would be regarded as a choice for instant severance of ties with France, including the instant cessation of French aid. Only

Guinea under the leadership of Sékou Touré rejected the constitution, whereupon the French attempted to make an example of that country by stripping it not only of French administrators but also of whatever physical capital could be taken.[5] By 1959, de Gaulle had come to feel that such vindictiveness was counterproductive; and in September of that year no obstacle was raised to the independence of the Mali federation (Senegal and the future Mali Republic) nor, in December, to that of Madagascar. This time there were no reprisals. In de Gaulle's words, "For everyone, the Community means effective independence and guaranteed cooperation."[6] For the French for the next twenty years, cooperation was to become the magic word in describing their new relationship with their former African colonies. With the exception of French Somaliland, which voted in 1958 to remain a French territory, every state (except Algeria) of the former French empire in Africa became independent in 1960.

Almost immediately cooperation was institutionalized (see Table 4.1). With each of the independent states (except Guinea), France concluded a series of separate treaties maintaining economic ties and cultural and educational aid, while a smaller number of the new states signed military technical assistance agreements, and eleven even agreed to bilateral defense agreements allowing for French military intervention (upon request) in their internal affairs. These important agreements had for France the undisguised purpose of maintaining its physical presence and deep-reaching influence in the affairs of Francophone Africa.[7]

These technical and cultural agreements provided for the supply of large numbers of French technical experts and teachers, known as cooperators ("*coopérants*"). During the colonial period the French had been very reluctant to train the native population so that they would be able to replace the French who had dominated governmental and civil administrations at every level. As a result, vast numbers of trained Africans were needed for even the lowest levels of administration. At the same time, large numbers of teachers were needed to raise the standards of education. But very quickly many African states began to feel that a disproportionate amount of French aid was being spent on paying the *coopérants*, who were criticized not only for preserving the dominance of the French language and culture but for more open intervention in local administration as well. By 1972 part of the disenchantment with the policy of "cooperation" evident throughout the sub-Saharan

TABLE 4.1
Major Cooperative Agreements with African States

Country	Foreign Policy	Defense	Strategic Raw Materials	Monetary, Economic, Financial	Civil Aviation	Cultural Cooperation	Higher Education	Technical Cooperation
Central African Republic	8-18-60	8-13-60	8-13-60	8-11-60	—	8-13-60	8-15-60	7-17-59
Congo-Brazzaville	8-15-60	8-15-60	8-15-60	8-13-60	—	8-15-60	8-15-60	7-23-59
Gabon	8-17-60	8-17-60	8-17-60	8-17-60	8-17-60	11-18-59	8-17-60	11-18-59
Chad	8-17-60	8-15-60	8-15-60	8-15-60	—	8-16-60	8-15-60	11-29-59
Madagascar	6-27-60	6-27-60	6-27-60	6-27-60	6-27-60	7-22-59	6-27-60 4-5-62	7-7-59
Senegal	6-22-60	6-22-60	6-22-60	6-22-60	6-22-60	2-4-60	6-22-60 8-5-61	9-14-59
Ivory Coast	—	4-24-61	—	4-24-61	4-24-61	4-24-61	4-24-61	4-24-61
Dahomey	—	4-24-61	—	4-24-61	4-24-61	4-24-61	4-24-61	4-24-61
Upper Volta	—	4-24-61	—	4-24-61	4-24-61	4-24-61	4-24-61	4-24-61
Niger	—	4-24-61	—	4-24-61	4-24-61	4-24-61	4-24-61	4-24-61
Cameroon	—	11-13-60	—	11-13-60	11-13-60	11-13-60	8-8-62	11-13-60
Togo	—	7-10-63	—	7-10-63	—	7-10-63	—	7-10-63
Mauritania	—	6-19-61	—	6-19-61	6-19-61	6-19-61	—	6-19-61

Mali	—	3-9-62	—	3-9-62	—	3-9-62	3-9-62	3-9-62
Guinea	—	5-22-63	—	5-22-63	—	5-22-63	–	5-22-63
Rwanda	—	12-4-62	—	12-4-62	—	12-4-62	12-4-62	–
Burundi	—	12-11-62	—	2-11-63	—	2-11-63	2-11-63	–
Zaïre	—	–	—	7-17-63	—	–	–	–

SOURCE: *Notes et Etudes Documentaires*, No. 3330 (October 25, 1966), p. 45.

states was due to this semicolonial presence which was regarded, for example, as one major cause of the anti-French riots in Madagascar in 1972. Even though the three principal reports to the French government on the nature of French assistance (the Jeanneney report of 1963, the Gorse report of 1970, and the Abelin report of 1975) all recognized the need to reduce the numbers of directly active teachers and administrators and to replace them with others who would train a generation of African teachers and administrators, the proportion of French aid devoted to the *coopérants* remained about 60 percent of all nonmilitary aid, while payments for equipment were only 30 percent.[8]

The economic agreements involved in "cooperation" also left France with wide powers of intervention. The African states remained within the franc zone, even though their economic weight was of minor importance in relation to the economic power of France; and thus the French were able to exert considerable control over the value of the African currencies—especially over credit and the money supply. This power became increasingly irksome as, with growing French integration into the European Economic Community after 1958, French commercial exchanges with the African states lessened. In 1958 the franc zone had supplied 27.6 percent of French imports and had purchased 37.5 percent of its exports. By 1971, those figures had fallen to 4 percent of French imports and 5.9 percent of French exports. Criticism of the power of the franc zone for its orientation of their economies, at a time when trade with France was losing its value, led both Madagascar and Mauritania to withdraw from the franc zone in 1972.[9] Even though the other African states recognized that the franc zone lessened the worry of running an unfavorable balance of trade and permitted easier commerce among themselves as a result of a common currency, they all felt that France seemed to gain unreasonably greater advantages—notably an increase, by half, of its foreign currency reserves and the ability of French firms to transfer currency easily among their African clients.[10]

The military agreements provided an excuse for the French policy of direct intervention in the internal politics of several of the African states. Two forms of military agreements were signed. The first, known as a defense agreement (*accord de défense*), permitted French military intervention—at the request of a local African government and with the approval of the French authorities—either for external defense or to maintain internal order. Eleven states signed these pacts in the 1960s, but only five still retained them in 1977 (Central African Republic,

Gabon, Ivory Coast, Senegal, and Togo). Djibouti (formerly French Somaliland) signed a defense agreement in 1978, after gaining its independence, as did the Comoros following a pro-French coup in 1978.

The second type of military agreement was the military technical assistance agreement (*accord d'assistance militaire technique*). This type of agreement permitted the French to train and equip the armies and police forces of the states that signed these pacts. The same eleven states that signed the defense agreement, as well as Upper Volta and Cameroon, signed the military technical assistance agreement. These agreements were also extended to the former Belgian colonies of Zaïre, Rwanda, and Burundi in the 1970s.

The period 1960–1964, which was a time of great political instability in the new African states, saw frequent French intervention in African affairs. On several occasions, they intervened to put down internal disorders, usually because of tribal disputes (Cameroon in 1960 and 1961, Congo-Brazzaville in 1960 and 1962, Chad between 1960 and 1963, and Mauritania in 1961). On other occasions, they went directly to the support of rulers threatened with overthrow, as when they put down a military move against President Hamani Diori of Niger in 1963 and when they put President M'ba back in power in Gabon after a military takeover in February 1964.

The basic reason for use of French military forces was stated in 1964 by Information Minister Alain Peyrefitte: "It is not possible that a few gunmen be left free to capture at any time any presidential palace, and it is precisely because such a menace was foreseen that the new African states have concluded with France agreements to protect themselves against such risks."[11]

French actions in Gabon provoked throughout Africa and the rest of the Third World an outburst of protest that persuaded the French drastically to reduce the number and the provocative character of their military interventions, as well as to streamline their military capacity for such actions. With the end of the Algerian war, it was decided to maintain only four large military bases in Africa—Dakar in Senegal, Abidjan in the Ivory Coast, N'Djamena (formerly Fort Lamy) in Chad, and Diego Suarez in Madagascar.[12] At the same time, as we saw in Chapter 3, the role of the *forces d'intervention* was clearly defined, especially in the defense of the remaining overseas possessions and in compliance with the defense agreements with the African states.

Between 1964 and 1974, the French military presence in Africa was kept as little visible as possible. Only two direct military interventions occurred. In November 1967, France sent troops to the Central African Republic to put down riots against Jean-Bedel Bokassa, the colonel who had seized power the previous year and established his credentials with the French by driving out the large Communist Chinese delegation that had become a major influence in his predecessor's government. From 1968 through 1971, it again sent troops to help restore order to chronically chaotic Chad.[13] At the same time, following the military takeover of Upper Volta in January 1966, the French obliquely threatened economic reprisals, even though they had declined to intervene on behalf of ousted President Maurice Yameogo. According to Jean Charbonnel, a member of de Gaulle's cabinet, the French were concerned that this coup would adversely "affect French aid and cooperation policy which can only be carried out in order and legality."[14] Perhaps the most significant expansion of the area of French activity in these years of self-effacement was the surreptitious shipping of arms to the Biafra secessionist forces in Nigeria in 1968; this action has been interpreted as an attempt to weaken that giant state and perhaps to weaken the lingering Anglo-Saxon influence in Africa as well.[15] Finally, the most criticized of French actions was their role, until 1977, as the principal arms supplier to South Africa, as well as that of grantor of licenses for manufacture in South Africa of complex military equipment. According to the U.S. Arms Control and Disarmament Agency, France supplied $450 million of South Africa's total imports of $622 million of arms between 1973 and 1977. By 1977 the South African military forces were believed to have in service 95 Mirage III fighter-bombers, 48 Mirage F-1 multipurpose fighters, 155 Aérospatiale helicopters, at least 4 Daphne class submarines, and possibly 80 AMK-13 infantry fighting vehicles.[16]

When Giscard d'Estaing became president in 1974, he realized that Soviet penetration into Africa was transforming a political situation that had permitted the French considerable independence of action with regard to both the Francophone countries and South Africa. The more radical of the former French colonies, notably Guinea and Mali, had turned to the Soviet Union for economic, technical, and military aid in the 1960s, but they had not proved tractable allies for the Soviet Union.[17] After the coup of 1963, however, the People's Republic of the Congo (Brazzaville) had been proclaimed a Marxist-Leninist state by the new president Alphonse Massamba-Debat; the same policy was followed by Marien Ngouabi, who seized power in 1968. It was through Brazzaville that the Soviet Union was able to send military supplies to the pro-Communist forces in Angola in 1975. But what was most disturbing to the new French president were the establishment of Marxist regimes in Angola and Mozambique, the leftward swing of the military regime in Ethiopia, and the Soviet influence in the Horn of Africa through Somalia. In 1978 in an important article in *Défense Nationale*, the semiofficial mouthpiece of the French military, General Méry, head of the General Staff, noted that the new Soviet influence created a climate of instability in Africa, and that it would be necessary for France to draw the line beyond which further destabilization would not be permitted.[18]

Giscard's first action was to abolish the much criticized General Secretariat for African and Malagasy Affairs and to retire to private life the shadowy activist, Jacques Foccart, who had been primarily responsible for French actions in Africa. But the housecleaning was more show than substance, since Giscard retained as his principal African adviser René Journiac who had been Foccart's right-hand man.[19] The new team was determined to be more flexible and more activist. First, it was necessary to handle those areas of tension that had arisen with the former French colonies. The administration of the franc zone was reorganized to permit a greater African share in decision-making, and increased credits were made available through it. New cooperation agreements were signed, including one with Guinea in 1975.

Second, an attempt was made to broaden French ties in Africa beyond those established with the former French empire. French pressure on its partners in the Common Market had led to closer economic ties, first with the former Belgian colonies (Zaïre, Rwanda, and Burundi) and then in the 1970s with the former British colonies. But Giscard sought closer bilateral relations for France itself. Following his visit to President Mobutu in Zaïre in 1975, France made a serious effort to become the principal patron of that crumbling state, in spite of the objections of Belgium. In 1979 alone, French economic aid to Zaïre was tripled. Military technical agreements were signed with Zaïre on May 22, 1974, and with Rwanda on July 18, 1975. French economic aid was also extended directly to the English-speaking states of Africa. By 1979, twenty-six states in Africa were receiving French aid, compared with the original thirteen in 1960, while the periodic conferences between France and its former colonies had been broadened to include twenty-four of the African states. Attempts had even been made, without much success, to strengthen French ties with the new Marxist regimes in Portuguese-speaking Angola and Mozambique.

Giscard's new activism in African affairs also took military form. From 1974 on, the French naval presence in the Indian Ocean was increased, with the stationing of fourteen warships in that region; these ships were based on Réunion, Mayotte, and five support points on smaller islands. In September 1978 a squadron of twelve Mirage fighters was sent to Djibouti, with the promise that they would eventually be handed over to the Djibouti air force.[20] The French sided with Mauritania and Morocco in their struggle with the Polisario guerrillas supported by Algeria, with the obvious intention of helping those countries retain control of the phosphate deposits of the former Spanish Sahara. In November 1977, troops were sent to free French citizens being held prisoner by the Polisario forces, an action presented as a symbolic gesture to put an end to the repeated kidnappings of French citizens. And in 1978 more open action was taken when French jets bombed Polisario bases on the territory of Mauritania.

The French have also intervened twice militarily in Zaïre. In 1977, when the rich mining province of Shaba (the former Katanga) was invaded by rebel forces based in Angola, the French airlifted Moroccan troops to help drive them from the province. In 1978, when a much larger incursion occurred and news was received of large-scale massacres of both Zaïre citizens and Europeans in the town of Kolwezi, seven hundred members of the Foreign Legion sent by France were able to drive out the rebels and bring Zaïre's own troops into order. But the latter action brought to light some serious weaknesses in the French intervention forces. The Foreign Legionnaires had to be flown in U.S. transport planes (thus indirectly involving the United States in the intervention), and they even had to borrow parachutes from Zaïre in order to be able to jump on Kolwezi. The French also discovered, as they had done in their skirmish with the Polisario, that they could suffer heavy losses—including the loss of aircraft—from the heavy weapons supplied to the African guerrilla armies by the Soviet Union through Algeria, Libya, or Angola.[21] Since the Kolwezi incident, the French have supplied to Zaïre 125 military advisers who concentrate on training the air force, tank troops, and parachutists.

Renewed French intervention in the Central African Republic and in Chad has been far more questionable. After French troops had prevented his overthrow in 1967, Jean-Bedel Bokassa created in the Central African Republic (which he converted into an empire in 1978) a viciously repressive regime, which the French, with some justification, were held to be maintaining in power by stationing French forces there. French public opinion appeared more shocked, however, by the accusation in 1979 that the French president and his family had in 1973 received gifts of diamonds worth $250,000 from Bokassa than by reports of Bokassa's repression. By then, however, the French government had cut off aid to Bokassa, after it had been proved he had murdered a group of schoolchildren for refusing to wear school uniforms. Then on September 20, 1979, French paratroopers helped carry through a coup d'état that restored to power Bokassa's cousin David Dacko who had been overthrown by Bokassa in 1966. Following the coup Bokassa attempted to take refuge in France, since he had retained his French citizenship; but after being kept in his airplane for several days in Evreux airport he was compelled to leave for exile in the Ivory Coast. When Dacko was overthrown by the army in September 1981, French troops made no attempt to aid him; and the French government announced that defense and other agreements would not be affected by the coup.

If French policy toward the Central African Republic (whose economy was in a shambles after the thirteen years of Bokassa's rule) was inept and at times unsavory, policy toward Chad was disastrous.[22] French colonial rule (1890–1960) had perpetuated in Chad the sharp north-south division of the country. The north, an arid region populated by nomadic or seminomadic tribespeople of Moslem religion, had been ruled directly by a military administration that continued functioning, even after independence, until 1964. The south, more densely populated and richer in agriculture (notably cotton) was either animist or Christian in religion and received both civilian administration and higher levels of education. At the time of independence in 1960, power was entrusted to François Tombalbaye, a Protestant from south Chad who solidified his own power during the following five years by a widespread series of arrests and expulsions and by the dissolution of all political parties except his own. Although on several occasions the French had used military force to put down unrest, Tombalbaye ordered their departure in 1964. When the military administrators in the north were replaced by civilian administrators appointed by Tombalbaye, the discontent of the northerners at new taxes and at discrimination against them led to a widespread peasant revolt and to the formation, in 1965, of the Front for the National Liberation of Chad (FROLINAT). FROLINAT's rapid progress in the north and center of the country persuaded Tombalbaye to ask de Gaulle to send the French army back into Chad. De Gaulle dispatched 3000 men in August 1968, but although their intervention stabilized the military situation, Tombalbaye increased his economic exactions and in 1973 began a paranoid campaign of arrest and cultural purification. Tombalbaye's arrest of General Félix Malloum, head of the general staff, finally provoked the Chad army to overthrow him in 1975, and although the French made no effort to save his regime, the new military council under Malloum once again ousted the French troops from the base at N'Djamena.

Three years later the French were asked back to stop the southward march of the FROLINAT forces who, with the help of arms and financial support from the government of Colonel Gaddafi in Libya, had won complete control of the north. The chaotic political and military situation from that point on illustrates the whirlpool into which the French can be sucked by this type of intervention. FROLINAT itself split. One small faction, under Hissène Habré, struck a bargain with General Malloum that permitted Hissène to become prime minister in August 1978. The main forces, under Goukouni Oueddi, continued to fight. The combination of a conservative general as president and a fiery reformer as prime minister proved unworkable, and in February 1979, combat broke out in N'Djamena in southwestern Chad between Malloum's and Hissène's forces. At this point Giscard ordered the French army to stay neutral. Hissène ousted Malloum from the presidency, but was compelled in November 1979 to accept the formation of a Government of National Union and Transition headed by FROLINAT leader Goukouni. By the spring of 1980 this fragile government had collapsed, however, and the forces of Goukouni and Hissène were fighting a desperate house-to-house battle through N'Djamena while the 1100 French troops remaining in their base attempted to keep functioning the few services that still existed. The correspondent of L'Express, looking around at the ruins of what was once Fort Lamy, commented in April 1980:

France continues to live through its purgatory here. It does not decide to leave because no one wants its departure, neither Hissène nor Goukouni. It remains because it feels itself responsible for the drama of its former colony and because it blames itself a little. It hangs on still because Paris judges that there remains something to be saved, even if it were only blocking the way to Tripoli or to Moscow.[23]

The last French troops were removed from N'Djamena in May 1980, part of them being transferred to the reactivated base of Bouar in the Central African Republic, where President Dacko proposed to use them in the training of his army. As for Chad, a communiqué from the Elysée palace declared, "French cooperation will begin again as soon as calm has returned."[24] To France's dismay calm returned in December 1980 with the complete defeat of the army of Hissène, when Goukouni's forces were joined by about 6500 Libyan troops armed with Soviet-manufactured T-54 and T-55 tanks, mortars, and rocket-launchers—and supported by bomber and fighter air cover. When, in January 1981, Gaddafi and Goukouni announced the "merger" of their two countries, the French government showed both frustration and humiliation. It explained that it had not intervened militarily because no French nationals were in danger and no request for aid had been received from the legitimate government of the country. (Goukouni had in fact requested Libyan aid in accordance with a treaty of alliance signed in June 1980. French aid to Hissène had of course remained covert, and as a result largely ineffective.) Although the French attempted to put pressure on Gaddafi by canceling oil exploration agreements that had been signed only one day before the merger, while attempting to reassure Niger, Senegal, and the Ivory Coast that they intended to continue to defend them against future moves by Gaddafi, it was evident to all observers that Giscard's policy in Africa had suffered a disastrous defeat; and President Mitterrand decided to reverse course by cutting off Hissène's aid, renewing relations with Goukouni and restoring the supply of French military equipment to Gaddafi. Gaddafi withdrew his troops from Chad at the end of 1981, at the request of Goukouni and under pressure from a number of African leaders.

Perhaps as the result of the vigor of the renewed policy of intervention under Giscard d'Estaing, French policy has come under strong African criticism, even from states like Nigeria, while the new regime in Mozambique has been scathing in its reproaches. Somora Machel's attack on France in July 1978 was an indictment of every French action in Africa since 1945:

> Those who presently occupy Mayotte [in the Comores]. . . have commit-ted the massacre of Sakiet Sidi Youssef, have massacred the Tunisian people when the latter wanted to get rid of the base in Bizerte, led a seven-and-a-half-year war against the Algerian people, have committed aggression against Morocco when it was offering a brotherly support to the liberation of Algeria, have backed the secession in Katanga and Biafra, have invaded Egypt when the Suez Canal was nationalized, have committed aggression against Guinea in 1972, have organized and armed the mercenaries who invaded Benin [January 1977], have supported ag-gression against the Saharan people, and attacked everywhere people who are fighting for their dignity.[25]

France in short had been cast as the principal villain in the mainte-nance of neocolonialism in Africa, or as the sole Western obstacle to the expansion into southern Africa of Soviet-supported liberation move-ments and into central and western Africa of Libyan- and Algerian-supported movements. To some extent, France's isolation was its own responsibility, since de Gaulle and Pompidou had both considered Africa—or at least French-speaking Africa—to be an area other Western powers should be warned away from. France's economic interest was clearly involved in maintaining this isolation, since it regarded Africa as of increasing importance for the supply to France of strategic raw mater-ials. The agreements signed with the African states in the early 1960s had included provision that France should have privileged access to a number of raw materials, notably uranium (needed not only for France's atomic weapons but also for its power stations) and titanium (for its air-plane industry). The agreements even provided that France should have the right in certain cases to put an embargo on supplies of these crucial materials to other countries. In November 1979 the German magazine *Stern* suggested that the whole purpose of France's African policy was to ensure its uranium supplies, noting especially the care with which France guards the mines of Arlit in Niger, France's main source of uranium in Africa.[26] As proof of the extent of French economic inter-ests in Africa, in addition to the soldiers and the *coopérants*, there were

280,000 French civilians in Africa in 1979, of whom 116,000 were in North Africa, 75,000 in West Africa, 51,000 in Central Africa, 30,000 in East Africa, and 6,000 in southern Africa.[27]

It is true, however, that Giscard d'Estaing made considerable effort to persuade France's European allies and the United States to collaborate in its African policies. The French had been the most enthusiastic promoters of the Convention of Lomé in 1975, which extended preferential economic relations with the Common Market to forty-six (increased to fifty-two in 1976) independent states in Africa, the Caribbean, and the Pacific. The French were able to persuade a number of economically advanced countries to join in a "western consortium" to shore up Zaïre, although they were disappointed at the extent of aid the United States was willing to give. Giscard failed, however, to get any response from his European allies when he invited powers "with African experience" to "involve themselves in the policy of stabilization and development in Africa."[28]

For the United States, this situation offers both advantages and problems. In the first place, France alone takes the opprobrium for the actions of its intervention forces, and the French public seems prepared to support its president, no matter how much external criticism his actions in Africa provoke. France alone of the Western powers possesses the freedom (and secrecy) of presidential power that makes such interventions possible. And the sphere of action chosen is, in the candid words of former foreign minister Louis de Guiringaud, "the only continent which is still the right size for France, still within the limits of its means. The only one where it can still, with 500 men, change the course of History."[29]

In the second place, however, the United States must recognize that this situation cannot continue indefinitely. The cost of economic aid and military intervention has become increasingly burdensome for France, particularly at a time when it is trying to reconstruct its conventional forces for potential use in Europe and is also trying to extend its economic aid beyond the traditional area of the French-speaking states. It is to be expected that France will have to cut back its ambitions in Africa considerably, posing the problem of whether the United States will be willing and able to take up part of France's burden. The threat of destabilization is especially strong in those states where France has been most active, since they are among the poorest states in the world. In

TABLE 4.2

French and Cuban Military Personnel in Africa

Country	French Military Personnel (1979)		Cuban Military Personnel (1978)
	French Intervention Forces	Military Technical Assistants	
Algeria			
Angola		90	21,000
Benin (Dahomey)			
Burundi		30 (1978)	
Cameroon		100	
Central African Republic	800		
Chad	1,100	85	
Congo (Brazzaville)		20	300
Djibouti	3,900 (plus 2 squadrons of Mirage III)	200	
Ethiopia			12,000
Gabon	500	200	
Guinea			200–300
Guinea-Bissau			70
Guinea (Equatorial)			20–30
Ivory Coast	400	120	

Libya		25 (1978)	100–125
Madagascar		50 (1978)	30
Mauritania	150	60	
Mayotte			
Morocco	2,000 (1978)	200	300
Mozambique			
Niger		60	
Réunion	2,000 (1978)		
Senegal	600	50	
Sierra Leone			100–125
Tanzania			20–30
Togo		100	
Tunisia		130	
Uganda			20–30
Upper Volta		20	
Zaïre		120	
Comores		30	
Mauritius		20	
Seychelles		20	
Total	11,450	1,730	34,000–34,500

SOURCE: *L'Express*, December 22, 1978, p. 35; *Le Nouvel Observateur*, May 22, 1978, cited in Lellouche and Moisi, "French Policy in Africa," p. 109.

1977, for example, the per capita gross national product in Chad was $130, in Mali $110, in Niger $160, in Upper Volta $110, and so on. The legacy of two decades of misgovernment in such states as the Central African Republic and Chad can only be an opening for revolutionary forces sympathetic to the Soviet Union or to Libyan-style liberation. It is therefore essential for the United States to develop with France effective methods of providing economic aid—in the short term, to help immediately the millions in central Africa who are literally starving and, in the long term, to break the vicious cycle of underdevelopment that has been perpetuated by chaotic political leadership.

Third, since Africa and the Indian Ocean are increasingly the focus of Soviet efforts at penetration, including use of its Cuban surrogate, some form of contingency military planning with France is vital. The most obvious points where such coordination is needed are in the Horn of Africa, between the American forces in Somalia and the French forces in Djibouti, and in the Indian Ocean, between the French naval forces at Réunion and Mayotte and American ships operating in the Indian Ocean. But on a broader scale the United States will have to determine whether it can support further military action by France similar to the many interventions it has undertaken since 1960. Greater support—political, financial, and logistical—for French actions could enable the United States itself to avoid the entanglement in internal African politics that could backfire, while safeguarding American interests on that continent, although at the risk of the French being considered America's Cubans!

5

France and
the Moslem World

The French have displayed ambiguous feelings about the
Moslem world. Historically, they have taken pride in the large number
of Moslems within their empire, which until the Second World War included the three states of the Maghreb (Tunisia, Algeria, and Morocco)
in northwestern Africa, and Syria and Lebanon in the Near East, as
well as large Moslem populations in sub-Saharan Africa. François Mitterrand could even declare proudly during the Algerian war, "the seven
million Moslem Algerians make France the second Moslem nation in
the world. This we must not forget."[1] Here was a vast body of millions of
people deeply impregnated with French thought and culture, modeled
by the civilizing mission of France which, in French opinion, had also
respected the high qualities of Islamic civilization. Cities like Marrakesh
or Fez in Morocco, where well-planned French suburbs existed har-
moniously side by side with the romantic confusion of the Moslem

medina, seemed a proof of the compatibility of the two civilizations. But the savagery of the Algerian war, followed by the flight of the entire French population from Algeria, seemed to give the lie to this notion of harmony within the French empire. And the hostility within France in the 1960s and 1970s toward the million or more Algerian and other North African migrant laborers was felt by many observers to have decided racist overtones.[2]

Regardless of their mixed feelings, the French have recognized since 1962 that for economic, political, and even military reasons it was essential for national self-interest that good relations be maintained with the Moslem states. From the end of the Algerian war in 1962 to the first oil crisis in 1973, France's principal interest lay in the states of the Maghreb, and in particular in Algeria. Economically, at least until the Algerian nationalization of its oil companies in 1971, the three Maghreb states played a far greater role in French trade than all the other Arab states combined. In 1965, total trade with the Maghreb was about three times larger than that with the other Arab states of the Middle East. In 1971, with the sharp reduction of French oil imports from Algeria, trade with the other Arab states exceeded that with the Maghreb for the first time.

During the 1960s, France had been predominantly interested in obtaining Algerian oil, which could be paid for by maintenance of the long-established export trade. Accounts with the Maghreb states, which were members of the franc zone, could be settled in francs; and large holdings of francs by those states acted to stabilize the franc internationally. In the booming economy of the 1960s, France also needed the labor of the large numbers of North African workers who were willing to take the poorly paid manual jobs that French workers increasingly shunned. Politically, good relations with the three former French colonies and especially with left-leaning Algeria promised a bonus in opening the Third World to French influence. De Gaulle was determined to shed the opprobrium that had attached to France as a result of its unwillingness to relinquish its colonial possessions, and nothing seemed more likely to guarantee France's standing with the anticolonialist powers than a harmonious relationship with the new Algeria. More old-fashioned motives subsisted for this French policy, however. The preservation of friendly relations with North Africa was not merely necessary for France's military production; it was a safeguard of the stability of sub-Saharan Africa where the French presence remained pervasive, and it revived a kind of "EurAfrica" – a geopolitical alliance that would open Africa and the Arab world to French influence. In a famous speech in 1964, Jean de Broglie, the secretary of state for Algerian affairs, stated France's ambitions quite openly:

> Certainly, while pursuing her policy of cooperation with Algeria, France defends certain interests and strives to counterbalance the tendency of that country to slide towards communism. But Algeria is also and especially the "narrow door" through which we are penetrating the Third World. A falling out between France and another North African state is only a simple bilateral tension. A falling out with Algeria would go beyond the limits of Franco-Algerian relations and would peril the efforts of our diplomacy in the whole world.[3]

Yet the area through which France aspired to expand its influence could easily become the region through which an attack might come. President Pompidou did not mince his words when he told the National Press Club in Washington, D.C., in February 1970:

> It is sufficient to look at a map and to see Europe, and where the Mediterranean is located, to realize that there is a way of attacking Europe from the south, that is to say, by the Mediterranean. And that consequently it is normal that the defense of Europe should be considered in this region as elsewhere. In the second place, it is equally sufficient to look at a map to see that France is directly interested in everything that happens in the Mediterranean.[4]

Thus, in France's relations with the Moslem states, economic interest, international political ambition, and military strategy were combined. It was not to prove a happy combination.

In the Evian agreements that concluded the Algerian war in 1962, de Gaulle had hoped not only to salvage a good deal of France's physical and human investment in Algeria but also to create a model relationship that would enable the ill feeling of the war years to be swept away and forgotten. It was a vain hope. For Algeria, the Evian agreements promised – in addition to full independence – French financial and technical aid, preferential trade relations with France, and social benefits for Algerian workers in France identical to those for French workers. In return, the Algerians made a number of promises that seemed even at the time of the signing to be almost certain to be infringed upon or later abandoned. Political and property rights of the European minority in Algeria were to be safeguarded. The French oil companies, which had an investment of over $1 billion in the Saharan fields, were to retain their property rights and be given a privileged status over foreign competitors in future development. France could continue to use its nuclear testing grounds in the Sahara for five years. France was to retain the naval base of Mers-el-Kebir for fifteen years.

Almost nothing remained of these agreements by 1971. First, fearing reprisals by the Moslem Algerians, especially after the 1962 rampage of terrorism by the *Organisation de l'Armée Secrète* (OAS), more than 650,000 settlers of European stock fled Algeria in 1962 alone. By 1965, more than a million had left. Violence against the *harkis* (the Algerian Moslems who had fought for the French) and their families caused 130,000 of them to flee to France. Thus the notion of a continuing presence in Algeria of a substantial French or European population was immediately disappointed.

Second, the Algerians soon pressed for rapid withdrawal of French forces from Algeria. The last troops of the French army were pulled out in 1964. In July 1966 the dismantling of the nuclear testing site in the Sahara was announced. And the naval base of Mers-el-Kebir was vacated in October 1966.

Third, the Algerian government began almost immediately to implement the program of nationalization it had declared as its goal as early as June 1962. The three French newspapers were nationalized in 1963. All foreign-held lands were expropriated in 1963, and all mining activities nationalized in 1966. In 1967, Algerian-owned banks were given a monopoly. For Algeria, however, control of its own oil industry was the most vital concern. Almost immediately French oil companies were required to keep half their receipts in Algeria. A seminationalization in 1965 increased the Algerian government's powers of taxation over petroleum production and their control of both new wells and storage facilities in Algeria. The French were only able to maintain their foothold by promising to buy Algerian oil for fifteen years at a higher price than the world market price and by investing about $200 million in Algerian industrial development. In 1971, however, the Algerian government decreed a total nationalization of natural gas and of the oil and gas pipelines and a 51 percent nationalization of petroleum. There followed a period of tension between the two countries, and popular passions ran high for a number of weeks until the French oil companies reached a settlement with the Algerians. That crisis ended French belief that they could engineer a Middle Eastern policy around an ongoing alliance with Algeria. In President Pompidou's words, "we do not give Algeria a priority in our cooperation but we do not exclude it either from the number of states with which we cooperate closely, and especially we abstain from any polemic."[5]

For its part, the Algerian government had complaints against France. It felt that France had not kept its promises concerning wine imports and the status of Algerian workers in France. The French had failed to keep their promise to import 8 million hectoliters of wine a year from 1962 on; and the Algerians, after complaining bitterly, began to replant their vineyards with other crops. The entry of 90,000 Algerian workers a year into France between 1964 and the end of 1967 disturbed the French government, who pressured the Algerians into agreeing to a restriction of the number to 35,000 a year from 1968 through 1970 and to 25,000 a year from 1971 on. Since the remittances from Algerians in France were thought to support one-fifth of the Algerian population, the Algerian government was embittered by this restriction on immigration, especially as efforts were made to replace them with other nationalities such as the Portuguese.[6]

The flow of French aid to Algeria was considerably curtailed as a result of this deteriorating relationship (Table 5.1). France also made a determined effort to reduce its reliance upon Algerian oil. Whereas in 1969 Algeria had been its principal supplier, by 1978 (Table 2.1) Saudi Arabia was by far its most important source, followed by Iraq, Iran, and Nigeria. In fact the ELF company, one of the two French oil companies operating in Algeria, had pulled completely out of that country in 1975 because of the difficulty of reaching any agreement through negotiation with the Algerian government.

The eclipse of French contacts combined with the revolutionary nationalism of the Algerian governments under Ahmed Ben Bella (1962–1965) and Houari Boumedienne (1965–1979) undoubtedly provided an opening for the Soviet Union to increase its influence, especially as it

TABLE 5.1

FRENCH AID TO THIRD WORLD COUNTRIES

Year	Total (millions of francs)	Percentage of GNP	Percentage of Aid to Algeria	Percentage of Aid to Tunisia & Morocco	Percentage of Aid to EAM	Percentage of Aid to DOM-TOM
1962	6,837	1.86	35.4	5.7	28.6	14.1
1966	6,508	1.22	13.0	6.3	32.3	35.3
1970	10,192	1.24	10.6	4.1	25.8	36.1
1975	16,902	1.16	4.8	6.1	22.2	38.7

SOURCE: Documentation Française, "Le Tiers monde et nous," *Cahiers Française* No. 167 (February 1977), pp. 49, 50.
NOTES: EAM—African and Malagasy States in the Franc Zone. DOM-TOM—Overseas Departments-Overseas Territories. French accounting includes DOM-TOM as recipients of foreign aid, which seems hard to justify in view of the fact that France also regards them as internal parts of French territory.

had provided the majority of the arms used by the Algerians in the later years of their war of independence. The greater part of Algerian military equipment was supplied by the Soviet Union from 1962 on, and included MIG fighters, Atoll and Styx missiles, submarine chasers and motor torpedo boats, and heavy tanks. (Only in 1969 did Algeria attempt to diversify its supplies a little by ordering 28 Fouga training planes and fifteen Puma helicopters from France.)[7] The Soviet Union was also the principal trainer of the Algerian armed forces, through some two to three thousand personnel in Algeria and through training programs for the Algerian air force in the Soviet Union.

Boumedienne, however, was determined not to permit one of the superpowers to dominate Algerian policy. The United States was welcomed in 1971 as an alternative customer for the oil and natural gas that France was giving up, and in 1974 the two nations resumed the diplomatic relations they had broken off in 1967.

Curiously enough, it was French refusal to follow American plans for a consortium of oil-consuming nations to counteract the concerted price rises by OPEC that brought France back into favor with the Algerians. The official government newspaper *El Moujahid* praised Foreign Minister Jobert's stand: "Without bothering about the attacks, which were indeed occasionally spiteful, and which in any case he was not spared, Michel Jobert was able to maintain the policy and the choices of France. He did it with a care for dignity and independence which in the end is one of the fundamental principles of the doctrine of nonalignment."[8] Jobert's talks in Algiers with Algerian Foreign Minister Bouteflika relaunched the collaboration between the two countries, thereby reviving, probably without foundation, the pipe dream of using Algeria as the key to a renewed French leadership of the western Mediterranean.

During the 1960s, before French disillusionment with Algeria had reached its peak with the oil nationalization, the French government allowed relations with Tunisia and Morocco to stagnate and even at times to become openly antagonistic, in spite of the pro-Western orientation of those two states.

Relations with Morocco had become stormy during the Algerian war, and there had been clashes between French and Moroccan troops on the border between Morocco and Algeria. But even after 1962 disagreements remained over Moroccan takeover of foreign-owned farmlands, transfer of French capital out of Morocco, and rights of French citizens living in Morocco. When the French government found the Moroccan minister of the interior implicated in the abduction and murder of a Moroccan revolutionary leader named Ben Barka who had taken political refuge in France, it broke diplomatic relations and suspended economic aid. But with the disillusionment with the Algerian tie, Pompidou decided in 1969 to swallow the discomfiture of the Ben Barka affair. He reopened diplomatic relations and, in agreements signed in 1970 and 1971, granted increased economic aid to Morocco. Finally, as we saw, in the late 1970s France sided openly with Morocco and Mauritania in their war with the Polisario guerrillas supported by Algeria and Libya.

The Algerian war caused sharp dissension between the French and the Tunisians who had recognized the provisional government formed by the Algerian FLN and permitted its forces to be supplied from Tunisia. The Tunisians accused the French of violating their borders from Algeria and demanded that the French (who had withdrawn all their troops in 1958 except those at the naval base of Bizerte) withdraw from Bizerte. In 1961, during demonstrations (orchestrated by the Tunisian government) against the French presence in Tunisia, French troops killed over 700 demonstrators. Only in 1963, when the Algerian war was over, did the French agree to withdraw from Bizerte. That year a new start was made in Franco-Tunisian relations with the signing of agreements on most matters of dispute between the two, including the status of Tunisian workers in France and the export of Tunisian goods to France. Aid and technical assistance to Tunisia were resumed at higher levels in 1963 and 1964. When, however, the Tunisians expropriated large areas of foreign-owned agricultural land in May 1964, the French reacted by stopping aid, canceling the import concession for Tunisian goods, and withdrawing some of their technical assistants.[9] As relations with Algeria deteriorated, however, de Gaulle and his successors sought a rapprochement with Tunisia. New cultural and technical agreements were signed in 1969. Loans were extended, and joint military exercises were held. It appeared that Tunisia was being granted the role Algeria had rejected—that of insinuating France into the counsels of the Third World; but in fact France had become the protector of this "most Western of Arab countries," a protector whose main function was soon to be to hold off the advances of Tunisia's increasingly unpredictable neighbor, Libya.

When Colonel Muammar Gaddafi had taken power in Libya in 1969, the French had moved at once to make themselves the primary European partner of the new régime. To the annoyance of the American government, they concluded the agreement to sell to Libya 110 Mirage planes (including 30 advanced Mirage IIIs) for about $400 million. As a result they provided planes that were used by Egypt (against the specific conditions of their sale to Libya) in the Yom Kippur war with Israel in 1973. After 1974, however, Gaddafi began to collide directly with what France regarded as its direct interests in Africa. In the growing disputes with Egyptian President Anwar Sadat after 1974, the French sided openly with Egypt and supplied it with arms and with military advisors, some of whom were present in 1977 when Sadat's forces mounted an invasion of the border regions of Libya. In Chad, too, where Gaddafi had sent troops and arms to the northern forces fighting against the French army, the French were in direct opposition to his expansionist policy. In the Western Sahara, the French were supporting the forces of Morocco and Mauritania and were at times taking direct action themselves against the Polisario guerrillas backed by Gaddafi. But the most threatening possibility of confrontation arose when Gaddafi turned against Tunisia.

Gaddafi had at first courted Bourguiba, and had even announced in January 1974 that the two countries had agreed to unite in a single nation called the Islamic Arab Republic. Under pressure from Algeria and Morocco, however, Bourguiba had first postponed the referendum on the union and finally, in 1975, had refused the merger. From that point, relations deteriorated, and France found itself increasingly in the role of protector of Tunisia against its powerful Libyan neighbor. By 1975, Gaddafi's 42,000-man forces were armed with a large variety of aircraft, missiles, tanks, and small naval vessels that had been acquired from Britain, France, and the United States between 1959 and 1973. Also, as a result of a $1 billion arms purchase from the Soviet Union concluded in May 1975, Libya was about to receive about 400 T-62 heavy tanks, 12 Tupolev bombers, and 6 Foxtrot class submarines. At this point the French also continued to supply Gaddafi with planes (including 16 Mirage F-1A fighters ordered in 1975 from Dassault) and with missiles (120 MM-38 Exocet ship-to-ship missiles ordered from Aérospatiale in 1975 and 232 R-550 air-to-air missiles ordered from Matra in 1975).[10] Against Gaddafi's forces Tunisia had an army of 22,000 armed with less than twenty planes.

In 1976, Gaddafi was responsible for an attempt to abduct the Tunisian prime minister; in 1977, the two countries quarreled over delimitation of their oil rights in the Mediterranean; and in 1978, Gaddafi called for the creation of revolutionary committees that would bring into power in Tunisia a pure Islamic government in place of Bourguiba's regime. France, for its part, promised Tunisia "firm and determined" aid as early as 1976. In 1978, the French general staff began studies of possible intervention by air in the Tunisian south in the event of a conflict there between Libyan and Tunisian forces. When in January 1980 a group of Tunisian dissidents trained in Libya attacked the oasis town of Gafsa in the center of Tunisia in the apparent hope of creating an insurrection that would lead to the overthrow of Bourguiba, the French intervened at once by sending helicopter-borne parachute troops and two Transall supply planes from their base at Pau in France and dispatching three cruisers toward Tunisia from Toulon. In addition, a number of Mirage surveillance planes were sent to the south of Tunisia where they neutralized the radio communications of the invading forces, while four Mirage F-1 planes were sent in a kind of symbolic overflight from Corsica to Djibouti. Although it was the Tunisian army that captured the invaders from Libya, their failure was blamed on France by the Libyan national radio. On February 4, 1980, undisturbed by Libyan police, crowds of demonstrators seized and sacked the French embassy in Tripoli and the French consulate in Benghazi, provoking the French to recall their ambassador and most of their diplomatic staff from Libya.[11]

Thus France's policy toward the Moslem countries of the southern Mediterranean has swung from an attempted alignment with the more radical and Soviet-leaning states of Algeria and Libya to a protective attitude toward the moderate republic of Tunisia and the conservative monarchy of Morocco. Although they have avoided any direct confrontation with Algeria, French policy has led them into open antagonism with Gaddafi—who attempted to penetrate the French sphere of influence and who saw his ambitions directly thwarted by the French—in Tunisia, Chad, the Central African Republic, the western Sahara, and even in Réunion (where Gaddafi called on the islanders to overthrow their French occupier). As a result of these conflicts, France has renewed its ties with Egypt, especially as President Sadat's relationship with Gaddafi turned to outright enmity; and it seems probable that French advisers were present at the brief Egyptian invasion of Libya's border regions in July 1977. French fears of Soviet penetration into the Mediterranean—and especially of the increasing activity of the Soviet fleets—have played their part in pushing the French government into reaffirmation of its support of Tunisia and Morocco.

Where de Gaulle had hoped that by withdrawing French Mediterranean forces from NATO as early as 1962 he would set an example of disengagement in the Mediterranean area and encourage the powers in that area to avoid entanglements with the superpowers, it had become clear in the 1970s that such a policy was infeasible and that, while the power of the United States was declining in the region, the strength of the Soviet Union was advancing with enormous speed. In fact, in the words of Le Monde editor André Fontaine, recognition of the "extent of the decline of American influence in the [Mid-Eastern] region, which is only the reflection of its universal decline," had become one of France's political truisms:

> Equalled, if not overtaken in the matter of nuclear armaments by the Soviet Union, whose copious fleets now move with complete impunity in the Indian Ocean and the Mediterranean, the United States can no

longer allow itself to put pressure by the mere presence of its forces on the outcome of an Israeli-Arab confrontation, as it did in 1967 with a quasi ultimatum of Johnson to the Kremlin and, in 1973, with the famous state of nuclear alert proclaimed by Nixon and Kissinger. It is out of the question for them to interpose, as they had without firing a rifle shot in 1958, in the Lebanese civil war. Nor is it possible for the CIA to mount an operation of "mobilization of the masses" comparable to that which had brought the shah, in 1953, from his brief Roman exile.[12]

In such a situation in the Mediterranean, as in the broader situation of the relative military powers of the blocs discussed in Chapter 2, it was clearly necessary, in French thinking, for France to take a larger role, and without declaring it openly, to take up part of the responsibility that the United States was proving itself incapable of handling.

When France expanded its role of influence (even as honest broker) among the Moslem states of the Near East and the Persian Gulf, the first casualty was its close relationship with Israel. Beginning in 1953 with the offer to Israel of twenty-four Ouragan fighters from the Dassault company, France had been Israel's principal arms supplier. In 1956, they had collaborated with Israel in preparation of the Suez expedition. During the Algerian war, Israel had been one of the few supporters of French intransigence. Even after the end of the Algerian war, when France was attempting to create a better relationship with the Arab states, it continued to supply Israel with advanced planes, and de Gaulle himself appeared to maintain his customary close personal relations with Israeli Premier David Ben-Gurion and with his successor Levi Eshkol. In 1967, however, after refusing to support Israel's demands for action to end the Egyptian blockade of the Gulf of Aqaba, de Gaulle ordered a halt on the shipment of arms to Israel, a ban that was imposed just two days before the Israelis launched their opening attack of the Six-Day War. Although this ban was partially lifted after the Israeli victory, a new total ban was imposed in January 1969 because the Israelis used French planes to attack Beirut airport in December 1968. And in a famous press conference on November 27, 1967, de Gaulle hinted that the Israelis were falling into the tendency to seek domination that he had seen in Roosevelt and the American people during the Second World War. "Some even feared [at the time of the establishment of Israel]," he said, "that the Jews—scattered up till then—but who had remained what they have always been, that is to say an elite people, sure of itself, and dominating, when once again gathered on the site of their former greatness, might change into burning and conquering ambition the very moving feelings they had developed over nineteen centuries." The Israeli occupation of Arab territory in 1967, he implied, was the outcome of this temptation to seek domination.[13] Neither Pompidou nor Giscard d'Estaing saw any reason to rebuild the bridges of understanding with Israel, especially as their policy was influenced increasingly by the sharp reality of French dependence upon Arab oil supplies and upon arms sales to the oil suppliers to pay part of the massive fuel bills that accompanied the price rises from 1973. At the same time, they continued to believe like de Gaulle that continuing Israeli occupation of Arab territory was an invitation to the two superpowers to become more actively involved in the Near East, which could only prevent France from reestablishing a position of influence itself. With Israel held at arm's length politically (although the embargo was quickly interpreted to apply only to the delivery of new Mirage planes), the French embarked upon a new courtship of the Middle Eastern powers.

The first move—the sale of the 110 Mirage planes to Libya in 1969—did not, as we have seen, lead to a prolonged honeymoon with Gaddafi. In fact, the use of those planes by Egypt in 1973 led France to end its embargo to Israel. Far more stable relations were achieved with the more moderate or conservative Arab countries. Economic relations flourished with Sadat's Egypt during the 1970s, with France purchasing petroleum products, cotton, and fruits and vegetables, and Egypt receiving arms, metal and chemical products, and machinery. French engineering companies were also invited to take part in building a textile factory, a thermal power station, several hotels, and a number of telephone networks. By 1979, France had become Egypt's second largest supplier, after the United States. With Saudi Arabia, to whom France had turned for over one-third of its oil supplies, relations were also harmonious. Not only was France awarded massive arms contracts, but it was also called upon for a number of large-scale engineering works such as dams, water treatment plants, and port facilities, and for apartment and hotel building. Similar economic relations were also achieved with Iran during the reign of the shah, although very few arms were sold. With all three countries, however, the French saw no possibility of displacing the United States from its predominant role, and remained in the background as an alternative partner, in case American influence declined. (They were not, however, invited to assume such a role after the Islamic revolution in Iran; and the exile in France of the Ayatollah Khomeini did not predispose him to seek French mediation or support. Relations in fact had become antagonistic by 1981 after France had granted political asylum both to former Iranian Premier Shahpour Bakhtiar and to former President Abolhassan Banisadr.)

It was with Iraq, the most radical of the Near Eastern Arab states, that France sought to achieve a privileged status. Saddam Hussein, who became president in 1979, had told a correspondent of *Le Monde* as early as 1972 that he wanted France to have relations with Iraq on a level with those of the Soviet Union, which had been the main support of the Baathist regimes since the revolution of 1958. Indeed, earlier in 1972, the Soviet Union had signed an important treaty of friendship and cooperation with Iraq, which gave the Soviet navy use of the port of Basra at the head of the Persian Gulf.[14] For the Iraqis, closer ties to France could have appeared a safe method of diversifying military supplies, gaining access to Western technology, and winning Western credits without compromising its anti-American posture. By 1979 some fifty French firms had been invited to Iraq to work on construction of its infrastructure. In 1977 orders were placed for 36 F-1C Mirage fighters and 100 Puma and Gazelle helicopters, and orders for tanks and missiles followed.[15] The most controversial agreement, however, was to sell Iraq a nuclear reactor. Although Iraq's original request for a graphite-gas reactor, which could easily have been turned to military nuclear purposes, was refused, Iraq was to be delivered a research reactor of the Osiris type, which would be under the inspection of the International Atomic Energy Agency of Vienna. However, the Israelis announced that they had discovered that not only was that reactor to function with a load of 15.5 kilograms of enriched uranium (which itself could be used for manufacture of an atomic bomb), but the French were also going to supply four times that amount of uranium, which would make it possible for Iraq to manufacture five atomic bombs. It seems probable that, as was recounted in the French review *L'Express*, Israeli agents took matters into their own hands in 1979 by destroying parts of the reactor while they were in workshops near Marseilles, and it is possible that Israeli planes, under the guise of being Iranian bombers, took the opportunity offered in 1980 by the Iraq-Iran war to bomb the power plant itself in Baghdad.[16] The reactor was finally destroyed by the Israelis in June 1981. Israeli feelings aside, the sale of the reactor to Iraq aroused suspicions in the United States and other Western countries that France was risking nuclear proliferation–specifically the possibility of the creation of the first Arab atomic bomb–in order to win favor with the radical Arab countries.

It is doubtful whether the French have gained what they had hoped from their solitary course in seeking to become the most trusted of the Western powers in the Arab world, and in particular in attempting to disassociate themselves from the policies of the United States. There is little evidence that France has begun to exert a political influence independent of the United States in the Arab world, and it is clear that the French have little to gain from the existence of anti-Americanism in certain of those countries. France's most successful relationships have developed with countries such as Egypt and Saudi Arabia with which the diplomatic contacts of the United States have been the most amicable. Attempts to work with the more radical of the Arab states have either been disastrous, as with Libya, or have at best not progressed beyond an increase in economic exchanges. Moreover, it is evident that the French have been unable to win any position of leverage in handling the broader international problems of the area, such as the Arab-Israeli conflict or the Iraq-Iran war. If they seek the cooperation of the superpowers, their attempts to create a consortium of great power decision-makers that would include France are usually deflected. Yet there are a number of positive features to France's somewhat maverick role in the Moslem world, just as there are to its actions in sub-Saharan Africa.

In the first place, the West's relationship with the Moslem powers is stronger for its diversification. It is highly undesirable, both politically and economically, for bilateral relationships to become exclusive. All Western countries need to diversify their sources of supply, notably of oil and natural gas, so that the sudden cessation of supply from one country will not cause a localized crisis within the Western system. Also, the countries of the Moslem world (and Israel) are stronger financially and technologically by diversifying their suppliers, and France has taken the lead in the West in encouraging this diversification. Second, by seeking closer relations with Arab countries closely linked to the Soviet bloc, France has offered them an opening to the West, without the direct implication of seeking to undermine Soviet influence for the benefit of the United States. This policy, while not immediately productive of direct political benefits to France itself, has the effect of supporting the nationalism within those states that is a safeguard against excessive demands from the Soviet Union. Third, there have been a number of occasions where the relatively small scale intervention of the French, especially in Tunisia and the western Sahara, has been effective in supporting pro-Western regimes, without the Western alliance as a whole becoming involved. As in the many French interventions in sub-Saharan Africa, there is no guarantee that the long-term interests of the West are served in any specific intervention. But, paradoxically, it is probably the lack of diversification of the intervening powers in such restricted areas that serves best. Fourth, the French have become increasingly aware that they must take a larger role in the use of sea power in the Mediterranean as the Soviet fleet augments its strength in that region. Augmentation of French naval presence in the Mediterranean could prove to be one of its most valuable contributions to Western security, without the necessity of the French fleet becoming reintegrated with NATO.

6

France and the Communist Powers

The policy of the Fifth Republic toward the Communist world has been (at least since President de Gaulle's visit to the Soviet Union in 1966) based on four principles. The first is that France had traditionally enjoyed and should seek to revive a privileged relationship with Russia—a closer partnership than that extended to any of the other Western powers. Second, France, having set the example of encouraging the disaggregation of the Western bloc by its withdrawal from NATO, should welcome any similar move by dissidents within the Soviet bloc; France, in short, stood firmly for a multipolar world. Third, France expected, as a result of the increasing ties between the Western and Soviet bloc countries and as a product of an internal liberalization following upon international détente, to see a progressive amelioration of political conditions and human rights within the Communist countries. Fourth, France needed, for economic self-interest, to develop closer commercial ties with the Communist countries—especially by the exchange of goods and services of high technology for raw materials and energy supplies.

As to the first principle, de Gaulle's somewhat wishful justification for having France receive special treatment from the Soviet Union was that Russia and France were the same as they had been for centuries, and that political systems—even revolutionary systems such as that of Soviet communism—were ephemera in the long perspective of relations between nations. "The visit to your country that I am ending," de Gaulle declared on Soviet television during his visit in June 1966, "is a visit that the France of always is paying to the Russia of always" (". . . *une visite que la France de toujours rend à la Russie de toujours*").[1] De Gaulle, of course, never made any secret of his detestation of the totalitarian system of government of the Soviet Union, but he constantly repeated that, as a result of history, the Russian people belonged to the "old Europe" that extended from the Atlantic to the Urals. In such a Europe, he implied, the consolidating force of the secular, cultural, and political ties of Russia and France would be of primary importance. Both Pompidou and Giscard d'Estaing, who were less prone than de Gaulle to refer to the Soviet Union as Russia, attempted to argue that it was the deep impregnation of each country with the other's culture that enabled them to work together regardless of their widely different political and social systems. Greeting Secretary General Brezhnev at the Château of Rambouillet in December 1974, Giscard d'Estaing could claim that the bonds of friendship and comprehension rested "on a profound knowledge of our respective cultures which, over the centuries, have mutually influenced and enriched each other," as well as on "our common struggles for the defense of liberty."[2]

It was, however, the determination of de Gaulle and his successors to seek accommodation with the Soviet Union beyond that offered by the United States that, the French leaders felt, had justified their immediate claim to Soviet understanding. The withdrawal from NATO, the attempts to reduce American influence within the European Community, the attempts to woo West Germany away from its dependence on the United States—all were tangible proofs of the harmony of French and Soviet policies. Above all, the French became the proponents of détente between the blocs, even before it became the *leitmotiv* of Brezhnev's foreign policy. The French were well aware that détente might well serve the national self-interest of the Soviet Union by permitting it to win recognition of the political status quo in Eastern Europe resulting from acceptance of the boundary changes that followed the Second World War and of the communization of the East European governments. Yet they believed that the eventual benefits of détente were worth the risk, and therefore proposed themselves as the obvious interlocutor with the Soviet Union when détente was to be negotiated. Giscard d'Estaing tried to persuade Brezhnev of this in the Rambouillet speech:

> Our policy of détente has never in fact been tied to the wish of adapting our foreign policy to transitory circumstances. It corresponds to a permanent orientation which led us to become, yesterday, the pioneers of a thaw in the relations of East and West, which has led us today to avoid the crystallization of new confrontations and which has led us to wish to pass together, with you, from the stage of détente to that of entente.[3]

It became clear how deeply rooted was this desire of the French to conceive themselves as the principal guardians of détente in the West when Giscard d'Estaing hurriedly arranged to meet with Brezhnev in Warsaw in May 1980 after the Soviet invasion of Afghanistan. In face of the accusation that he was, in the words of Le Figaro, "bringing the USSR out of the moral ghetto into which its aggression against Afghanistan had placed it in the eyes of the non-Communist world," Giscard d'Estaing justified himself by arguing the need to save détente. "In a situation of tension, it is necessary for the responsible world leaders to know exactly the others' point of view. Many of the catastrophes of world history in the course of the last fifty or hundred years were due to the lack of communication or explanation between the main world leaders."[4]

It is doubtful whether the French have gained any sort of special influence with the Soviet leadership; certainly they have not gained a privileged relationship. As early as 1975, Raymond Aron wrote that such a relationship was a mirage that existed in the vocabulary of French but not of Soviet politicians. Aron felt that the Soviet Union needed nothing from France, especially after it had opened a dialogue both with President Nixon and Chancellor Brandt, and that France had gained nothing from the Soviet Union—no modification of its international policy, no restraints on the actions of the French Communist party at home. The total lack of results for France stemming from the Warsaw meeting, Aron wrote in 1980, confirmed the inability of France, acting alone, to cause any change in Soviet actions.[5]

The second basic principle in French policy toward the Communist powers was the desirability of encouraging the break-up of the Soviet bloc. De Gaulle was particularly conscious of the value of a Sino-Soviet split. As early as 1959, in an extraordinary press conference, he implied that the conflict between the Soviet Union and China was inevitable because it was both racial and geopolitical:

> Doubtless, Soviet Russia, although having helped Communism to be-come established in China, realizes that nothing can change the fact that she is herself Russia, a white European nation which had conquered part of Asia and that she is very well endowed with land, mines, factories, and other wealth, while she is confronted with the yellow multitude which is China, numberless and wretchedly poor, indestructible and ambitious, building by dint of sacrifices a power which cannot be measured in ad-vance and looking around at the expanses over which she must one day spread.[6]

When in January 1964 he decided to recognize the Communist gov-ernment of China, de Gaulle made it clear that he was not only renew-ing contact with a country with which France had had "mutual and deep sympathy and respect" but also recognizing the existence of an in-dependent center of power in Asia whose national self-interest would cause it increasingly to pull away from its doctrinal solidarity with the Soviet Union. The French did not expect many dividends from this action, and other than a small increase in trade, they have received few. The important result was, in French eyes, a contribution to the prolifer-ation of poles of power, and thus to the lessening of the confrontation of power blocs in the world. In Europe, the greatest hope was placed on Rumania and Poland as possible defectors from the Soviet bloc and on Yugoslavia as an actual defector. But great care had to be exercised to avoid creating tension with the Soviet Union by surpassing the bounds of the permissible. Hence, during the mid-1960s, concrete agreements on such matters as cultural exchanges and scientific collaboration as well as an increased trade were preferred to more open blandishments.[7] When de Gaulle visited the East European states such as Poland in 1967 and Rumania in 1968, his welcome may have been heartwarming but it had little practical result. It was with West Germany rather than with France that East European states wanted to reach agreements of substance; this became evident when Chancellor Brandt embarked upon his *Ostpolitik*. French willingness to accept the borders of Eastern Europe and to come to a *modus vivendi* with the Communist regimes there was of minor significance compared with a West German change of heart. Moreover, the Soviet invasion of Czechoslovakia in 1968 put an end to that promising movement for independence within the Soviet bloc and dashed French hopes for a disintegration of the Warsaw Pact.

Third, it thus became necessary to place greater emphasis upon the transformation of Communist societies from within, under the stimulus of greater contacts with the Western countries, most notably with France. In 1962, de Gaulle merely conceived that the West should hold up an example that the Communist countries would wish to emulate— "in the face of the totalitarian system drawn up against the West...to offer the other camp the striking and attractive demonstration of a way of life which is more fruitful than theirs and to hasten that transformation in them, that has perhaps already begun, which is the true chance of peace."[8] In 1968, after the invasion of Czechoslovakia, de Gaulle declared that "by beginning to knit with the countries around the Vistula, the Danube, and the Balkans the special ties which for many centuries have bound us to them in so many respects [the French] were intimating to the great Russian people...that all of Europe expects from [Russia] something quite different and much better than seeing it shut itself in and chain its satellites behind the walls of a crushing totalitarianism."[9] And when, just a few days before his trip to Warsaw in 1980, Giscard d'Estaing was asked whether détente was leading to the democratization of the Communist countries, he could see positive results:

> Does détente contribute to the evolution of the Socialist societies? My reply is yes. That has been the case in Eastern Europe. If you take countries like Hungary, Poland, in spite of their great economic difficulties, these are societies that have evolved in depth. I am not speaking of their political orientation. The case of the Soviet Union is different, because the Soviet Union has never known a regime of a democratic type and does not have the basic structures that would enable such a regime to develop by itself. But, in the relations of the Soviet Union with the Western countries, there also have been important results.[10]

And it was precisely with this kind of hope that détente would open up the frontiers of Eastern Europe to the life-giving influences of the West that Giscard d'Estaing signed the Declaration of Helsinki at the end of the European security conference in July 1975, displaying considerably more enthusiasm for its outcome than had been shown by President Pompidou. Even Giscard, however, thought it necessary to remind the Russian leaders during his state visit the following October both that the Helsinki agreements included a program of implementation (by which he certainly referred to the agreements on human rights and easier human contacts across the frontiers) and that he was convinced that the Soviet Union intended to carry out their promises.[11] And by the time of the 1981 election campaign, it was evident that Giscard and his foreign minister, François-Poncet, had dropped any pretense that détente was still a viable concept in dealing with the Soviets. His challenger, Socialist François Mitterrand, had established a long record of denunciation of Soviet expansionism, and in particular, had immediately condemned the invasion of Afghanistan. Perhaps for this reason, the Soviet press was careful to praise Giscard for his positive approach to East-West relations, while expressing disquiet about the future of détente under a Mitterrand presidency.

The French people as a whole have displayed considerable cynicism about these hopes of their governments. In a survey of a thousand people interviewed in May 1980, those questioned showed a deep distrust of Soviet motives and of the value of détente. Asked whom the policy of détente had profited the most during the past ten years, 52 percent said the Soviets, 32 percent the West. Asked what the Soviet motives were in pursuing a policy of détente, 36 percent said that it was due to a "sincere desire to preserve the peace," while 59 percent said it was "to lull the Occident and to increase their zone of influence in the world." Curiously enough, this interpretation did not push the majority closer to the Western alliance. While 40 percent said that France should strengthen its solidarity with the West and only 6 percent wished to move closer to the Soviet Union, 44 percent called for France to pursue a neutralist policy![12]

The fourth and most promising goal of rapprochement with the Communist powers was to find new markets for French manufactured goods and services and new sources of raw materials. In a sense, French amour-propre was also involved. In the first years of the de Gaulle presidency, when the United States was refusing to welcome France into the club of the nuclear powers, it was flattering to be recognized by the Soviet Union as a highly advanced technological power, possessor of the industrial mastery that would enable it to export its engineering skills as well as its traditional luxury goods. The Soviet delegates to the Franco-Soviet committee—created in 1966 to supervise the high-level policy decisions concerning economic, scientific, and technical exchanges—were enormously flattering in their appreciation of the value of French technology for the Soviet Union; and such decisions as the adoption of the French system of color television for use in the Soviet Union appeared to be a practical outgrowth of their admiration. The French were well aware of the difficulties and risks of attempting to increase trade with the Communist bloc countries. Negotiations were always long and painful. Frequently, large-scale credits had to be made available at favorable terms of interest. Sometimes, in the case of the construction of complete factories, a guarantee had to be given that part of their production would be purchased by France. For example, when Poland signed a contract in 1972 for a 335-million-franc cable factory whose production would exceed the internal needs of Poland, the French had to agree to purchase part of the excess production.[13] Nevertheless, it was felt that these countries represented an untapped and growing market in which France's foreign policy initiatives would open the way for economic penetration on a favored basis.

To what extent have these expectations proved to be self-delusions? The diplomatic trappings of a privileged relationship were established fairly easily, beginning with de Gaulle's dramatic and well-publicized state visit of June 20 to July 1, 1966. De Gaulle was received with a pomp unequalled in the reception of any previous Western visitor, and he was given what seemed unparalleled access to the Russian people. He gave a speech at the University of Moscow, a talk on Soviet television, and a speech from Lenin's balcony in Moscow. He was taken to the Soviet space center at Baikonur to see the launching of a rocket and to factories in Siberia and the Ukraine. At the end of the visit, a Franco-Soviet declaration was signed providing for the development of economic, scientific, technical, and cultural collaboration. Other high level meetings followed. Since their frequency and significance were closely related to the level of tension between the blocs, they are worth listing chronologically. The increase in the number of meetings since 1966 is remarkable in view of the sparsity of the contact at the summit between 1944 and 1966, as shown below:

Summit Meetings of Franco-Soviet Leaders

1944. November 30–December 16. General de Gaulle to Moscow as head of provisional French government. Meetings with Stalin.

1956. May 15–22. Visit to Moscow by Premier Guy Mollet.

1960. Visit to France by Soviet Party Secretary Nikita Khruschev.

1966. June 20–July 1. Visit to Soviet Union by President de Gaulle. Talks with Brezhnev, Kosygin, and Podgorny. Signing of Franco-Soviet Declaration.

December 1–9. Premier Kosygin visits France.

1967. July 3–8. Visit of Premier Pompidou to Russia. Signature of several economic and technical agreements.

1970. October 6–13. President Pompidou visits Russia. Signature of Protocol on Political Consultations.

1971. October 25–30. Party Secretary Brezhnev visits France. Signing of Principles of Cooperation between USSR and France.

1973. January 11–12. Nonofficial visit by President Pompidou to Russia (Minsk).

June 25–27. Brezhnev's working visit to France (Rambouillet).

1974. March 11–13. President Pompidou visits Russia (Pitsounda).

December 4–7. Brezhnev's working visit to France (Rambouillet).

1975. October 14–18. State visit by President Giscard d'Estaing to Russia. Signing of Declaration on Further Development of Friendship and Cooperation.

1977. June 20–22. State visit by President Brezhnev to France.

1979. April 28–29. Giscard d'Estaing visits Russia. Signing of Program of Development and Cooperation.

1980. May 18. Meeting of Giscard and Brezhnev in Warsaw.[14]

Thus, it can be seen that, since the de Gaulle visit in 1966, summit conferences between the heads of government of France and the Soviet Union have become almost institutionalized, just as the French wished. The exchange of views has dealt with many controversial topics, the invasion of Afghanistan being the most divisive. Others have included the Vietnam War (in 1966), the Near East (on almost every occasion), the West German *Ostpolitik* (in 1971), and the French intervention in

Africa (in 1977). In no case, however, was there a sign that either government had altered its policies, and on every occasion the French press was careful to note that the meeting was "presented as a success," with the journalists testing the level of friendship by who took whom to the airport. Whereas for Giscard the very fact of the meetings was significant, if only in keeping open lines of communication, the Warsaw meeting in 1980 cast doubt on his basic assumption by indicating that the refusal to meet is in itself a form of political pressure.

The specific results of the various protocols signed have not been far-reaching, even though the Soviet newspaper *Izvestia* could praise them as the expression of "the common desire of the two states to unswervingly follow the course of concord and cooperation, promote diverse ties in every possible way, and do everything in their power to strengthen security in Europe and throughout the world."[15] The agreements at the end of de Gaulle's visit in 1966 led to the establishment of a large number of consultative technical committees for such fields as medicine, space, and meteorology in addition to the committees implementing the cooperation agreements. The Protocol on Political Consultations of 1970 contained fairly vague promises to consult more frequently on matters concerning "détente, cooperation, and security." The Principles of Cooperation of 1972 expressly noted their intention to collaborate closely in Europe and in the United Nations; but within a few months the French were complaining privately at the lack of any real Soviet interest in French opinions. Partly for this reason, the various agreements signed by Giscard d'Estaing in 1975, 1977, and 1979 included further declarations of determination to consult more fully, with the declaration of 1979 calling "in principle" for summit meetings once a year. But it was evident, by the manner in which the French prepared for the summit meeting of May 1979, that they had concluded that success was better measured in terms of economic rather than political gains. As the London *Economist* pointed out, "the French made it clear that continued good political relations—which to the Russians mean French reticence on sensitive issues such as human rights—depended on big new orders for French companies."[16]

French relations with the other Communist countries have progressed in pace with the Franco-Soviet rapprochement, and no faster. They have certainly not provoked scission within the bloc. First steps toward a closer relationship were taken from 1964 to 1966, when French cabinet members paid a large number of visits to Eastern Europe to prepare for the establishment of bilateral committees for technical and scientific cooperation and to negotiate commercial agreements. The French were particularly pleased that, with the dropping in Rumania of compulsory Russian language study, French became the first foreign language chosen by the majority of students.[17] De Gaulle's first state visit to an East European country was to Poland where, in spite of a warm popular reception, the Polish Premier Wladislaw Gomulka warned him bluntly that Poland had learned in the prewar years to consider France unreliable as an ally.

[The Franco-Polish alliance] was not able to protect either Poland or France from the catastrophe of defeat and occupation by Hitler. Alliance with the Soviet Union, together with the treaties of friendship, cooperation, and mutual assistance concluded with the Socialist states of Central, Eastern, and Southern Europe...is the cornerstone of the policy of the Polish People's Republic and the principal guarantee of her security.[18]

His trip to Rumania, which was to have cemented the ties between two Latin nations, proved something of a debacle because he had to break off his stay to fly back to Paris to handle the student riots and worker strikes of May 1968. The Soviet invasion of Czechoslovakia in August of that year completed the blocking of de Gaulle's opening to the east.

Pompidou's approach was more realistic and more cautious and was based on a determination to let the Soviet leaders know that the French and Soviet systems were different and ultimately irreconcilable. When welcoming Brezhnev in 1971, he told him in his first remarks:

We do not pretend to ignore the fundamental differences which separate our economic and social systems and, consequently, our political institutions. Your eminent position among Soviet leaders illustrates the role of the party in the organization of the USSR and consequently in its politics. It is not less certain that France adopted, in the final instance at the appeal of General de Gaulle, very different institutions, that its economic and social organization, even if it is far from corresponding to the theoretical image of liberal capitalism, links it to the Western world, and that its alliances, like the active part that it takes in the construction of Europe within the framework of the communities, are an integral part of its policy.[19]

Pompidou was no more inclined to make dramatic gestures toward Eastern Europe than he was toward the Soviet Union, although the slow, cautious conclusion of detailed agreements continued, especially as the Soviet Union seemed inclined to recoup its loss of prestige following the Czech invasion by permitting its allies to conclude innocuous agreements with the Western countries.

Giscard d'Estaing made a number of efforts to revive the momentum of the reconciliation with Eastern Europe, but as in the relations with Russia, he made clear that economic self-interest and political rapprochement go together. He particularly sought to create strong bonds with the regime of Edward Gierek in Poland with whom he was in agreement, in Gierek's words, that "economic ties are the material basis of the total development of Franco-Polish relations. These ties create the infrastructure for the peaceful coexistence between states with different systems in Europe and the world."[20] The price Giscard was willing to pay was evident in the French promise in 1975 of a 7-billion-franc ($1.59 billion) loan to Poland over a three-year period. There is no doubt that during the Giscard d'Estaing presidency trade relations improved notably, even though there was a slackening of the pace in 1978 (Table 6.1). But it is also clear that France, like the United States and West Germany, has to some extent become the prisoner of the countries to which it has made these enormous loans. Medium-term commercial credits, which represented the primary method by which France enabled the Communist countries to purchase its exports, had reached an accumulated total of 16.2 billion francs ($3.6 billion) for the USSR, 6.6 billion francs ($1.46 billion) for Poland, and 6.3 billion francs ($1.4 billion) for Yugoslavia. In order to extend these credits, French banks were authorized to borrow on the international money markets, and many financial analysts had begun to question whether this form of commerce made economic sense, especially with countries like Poland that appeared unlikely in the long run to be able to repay their debts. Marcel Théron, a vice-president of the Bank of France, suggested an even more ominous interpretation when appearing before a Senate committee headed by Socialist senator Edgard Pisani: "The plan which the USSR is currently putting into practice envisages first an increase of loans from the West and then the strengthening of its Army. That is to say that, in principle, we are indirectly in the act of financing the increase of the Soviet military potential. Perhaps one day the USSR will come to pay its debts in kind!"[21] In general, however, the greatest fears in France were of the danger of borrowing from the developed countries and the oil exporters in order to make loans to countries with enfeebled economies. The economic distress of Poland, accentuated by the disputes of its labor unions and the government in 1980, appeared serious proof of the dangers France was running.

The French approach to relations with the Communist countries poses several important questions. Is it of value to the West for a member country to possess privileged access to consultations with the Soviet Union and the other Communist countries, assuming that such a position was genuinely attainable? In times of genuine détente between the two alliance systems, that is to say in times when concrete negotiations are bringing about realistic agreements, a position of interlocutor as conceived by de Gaulle—and to a lesser degree by his successors—does not have much value. The Soviet Union has always chosen to negotiate directly with the United States in such a situation. And in times of tension, the position of interlocutor is either of little value or even counterproductive. No intervention by one single member of the Western alliance is effective in cases of internal conflict within the Communist bloc. Mediation, like that of Giscard's Warsaw meeting in 1980, serves only to emphasize Western disunity of strategy, if not of purpose.

Can closer links be created between peoples, regardless of the fact that their governments have opposed concepts of politics, economics, and society? The answer seems to be a modified affirmative, within very strict limits. Exchanges of persons for scientific or technical purposes have advanced most rapidly. Cultural exchange has been slower, but still worthwhile. The free movement of peoples for the purpose of mutual acquaintance, for the kind of osmosis that was the genuine purpose of Franco-German youth exchanges from the 1960s on, was virtually unthinkable with the Communist countries. Yet it was precisely through that kind of exchange, resulting in acquaintance with the action of a free society, that the French envisaged the eventual transformation of the Communist societies from within. Nevertheless, the gains in breaking through the barriers have been real, and should be encouraged.

Finally, does increased trade with the Communist countries serve the interests of the West? The answer again must be qualified. Access to sources of energy and scarce raw materials is useful in diversifying supply. Access to new markets for manufactured goods helps mitigate the

TABLE 6.1

FRENCH TRADE WITH SELECTED COMMUNIST COUNTRIES
(Millions of Francs)

	1974		1975		1976		1977		1978		1979	
Country	Exports	Imports	Exports	Imports	Exports	Imports	Exports	Imports	Exports	Imports	Exports	Imports
USSR	3,151	2,819	4,898	3,306	5,312	4,386	7,237	5,676	6,551	5,626	8,532	7,619
Poland	1,796	1,261	2,681	1,511	3,580	2,060	2,369	2,091	2,264	2,442	2,574	2,345
Rumania	882	766	866	746	1,238	984	1,337	895	1,595	1,046	2,354	1,465
Czechoslovakia	505	421	685	445	772	520	611	635	640	633	643	710
East Germany	455	603	774	701	1,016	897	596	789	752	1,001	1,537	918
Hungary	557	364	708	395	619	474	785	584	924	546	894	653
Bulgaria	360	137	523	156	489	239	606	213	420	255	602	292
China	769	878	1,610	742	1,604	928	467	952	890	1,016	1,442	1,388
Total (World)	220,213	254,651	223,362	231,269	266,228	308,012	311,550	346,207	344,594	368,401	414,677	457,128

SOURCE: INSEE, *Annuaire statistique, 1980*, pp. 628–30.

deficits in the balance of payments due to the high price of oil imports. But two weaknesses are evident. First the supply of high technology and especially the sale of complete factories can in the long run lead only to a drying up of the markets for manufactured goods and may even lead to new sources of competition. Moreover, there is a very fine line between peaceful and nonpeaceful utilization of certain exports, such as computers or nuclear facilities. Second, the financing of exports by low-interest credits to the Communist countries not only gives those countries greater flexibility in planning their own internal expenditures (e.g., by increasing military spending) but also ties the Western countries to their economic survival, and thus to the political viability of the Communist regimes. In this respect, however, France's policy has been little different from that of the United States.

7

France and
the Western Alliance

No power of France's size, perhaps not even a superpower, expects the kind of independence that de Gaulle at times appeared to be demanding for France. He could tell the world sardonically that it should not be surprised that "France should wish to be itself externally, that it should not give up being France even in Europe, even in the world. France has chosen once and for all to be France, and I invite everyone to put up with it."[1] Yet, as de Gaulle was well aware, this myth of independence in policymaking could only be cultivated as long as France was secure in its alliances. And, with considerable skill and occasional brutality, he set about moulding those alliances to serve as the underpinning of his wider world ventures. This alliance structure, which was in most essentials preserved by Pompidou, Giscard d'Estaing, and Mitterrand, had three main elements—the Franco-German partnership, a European Community responsive to French economic and political wishes, and an Atlantic community, in which the United

States would be the guarantor but not the mentor of a European Europe.

Perhaps the greatest achievement of the diplomacy of France and Germany in the postwar period was to overcome the age-old hatred between two countries that had, as the French never tired of repeating, provoked three major wars between them in less than a hundred years. In 1945, distrust of Germany was part of the very fabric of French life. In a sense, the German occupation of France during the Second World War had been even a more searing experience for most French people than the sufferings of the First World War, although the losses in lives had been considerably less—half a million compared with one and a half million in the First World War (and 140,000 in the Franco-Prussian war of 1870–1871). It was, however, the ubiquitous experience of the occupation, with the forced transfer of labor to Germany, the economic exploitation, the concentration camps, and such atrocities as the massacres of Vercors and Oradour, that had left so many with what appeared to be an unrequitable revulsion against the Germans. For at least twenty years after the Second World War, this psychological barrier between the French and German peoples was a major factor of international politics, and it would be unrealistic to think that, even in the reconciliation of the 1960s and 1970s, some residue of distrust did not remain, especially at times when there seemed any possibility of a reunion of West and East Germany.[2] Nevertheless in spite, or perhaps because, of the depth of the alienation between the two countries, imaginative efforts were undertaken to bridge the gap. De Gaulle himself, as early as 1945 and 1946, proclaimed the necessity of a reconciliation of the peoples on both sides of the Rhine, with the ultimate objective of creating "a western grouping, with the Rhine, the Channel, and the Mediterranean as arteries," and of making this organization "one of the three planetary powers, and should it one day be necessary, the arbiter between the Soviet and Anglo-Saxon camps."[3] The initiative for this reconciliation had to come from the French, and in the period of the occupation of Germany and the early years of the Bonn Republic, the French did in fact create bonds that were not merely economic and political but also personal. Among the many achievements of these years were the creation of the University of Mainz by the French occupation authorities, the "twinning" of 115 German towns with similar towns in France, and exchange visits of every type of private group. By the mid-1950s bonds of understanding that had been created on an individual level had begun at least to dilute the venom left by the German occupation.[4] At the same time, an institutional framework had been created in which the French and Germans could work together. German entry into both the Western European Union and into NATO in 1955 brought the French and German armies together in alliance. But above all, the common effort of creating the European Coal and Steel Community in 1952 and the EEC and Euratom in 1958 enabled them to cooperate in formation of organizations in which their national sovereignty would be abrogated to some degree but in which the presence of other members (Italy, Belgium, the Netherlands, and Luxembourg) would calm the tensions that might arise from a completely bilateral arrangement. The significance of participation in these communities will be discussed in detail later; but it is essential to remember that every effort to improve bilateral relations was able to draw strength from the collaboration that had been established within the broader West European grouping. (Curiously enough, one of the most interesting organizations promoting faster collaboration was not the product of governmental action but a pressure group founded to stimulate the governments to more courageous steps of integration. Jean Monnet's Action Committee for the United States of Europe, founded in 1955, was a private committee, composed of leading politicians and trade-union leaders from the EEC countries, that not only pressured the governments to adopt specific measures of integration but provided a forum in which French and German decision-makers came to know and trust each other.)

From the very moment of his return to power in 1958, de Gaulle determined to go beyond the fecund contacts that were growing within the European Community and to base his European policy upon the creation of a close Franco-German alliance (or perhaps what many of his opponents called a Franco-German axis). It is possible that de Gaulle had envisaged, for a time, the conversion of EEC into a political union dominated by France, although that would have been a "Europe of states" rather than a supranational union; but his proposals for such a union had been rebuffed in 1962 by the Dutch and Belgian governments. He therefore turned to German Chancellor Konrad Adenauer to create in a Franco-German alliance the base for political action that had eluded him in the EEC. Although Adenauer had at first expressed considerable apprehension about the fact that de Gaulle had returned to power as the result of an army coup in Algeria, he was completely won over by de Gaulle's charismatic courtship. Dramatic state visits prepared the way for the new relationship—Adenauer's visit to France in July 1962, and the return visit of de Gaulle to Germany that September. Symbolism was rich during these meetings. Adenauer joined de Gaulle in attending mass at Rheims Cathedral and watched a march-past of French and German troops. De Gaulle spoke in German to the steelworkers of the August-Thyssen works, telling them: "For Charles de Gaulle to be here, and for you to give him this cordial and moving welcome, our two peoples must truly trust each other." He even admitted that one of his own ancestors was German. In this atmosphere of reconciliation, de Gaulle and Adenauer agreed to draw up a treaty of cooperation, which they signed in January 1963, promising regular consultation between all levels of the French and German governments. In particular, they agreed to "consult each other on all important questions of foreign policy prior to any decision, and above all on matters of mutual interest, with a view to reaching, insofar as possible, a similar position."[5]

This treaty could in fact have been very far-reaching in its effects had it been implemented as de Gaulle intended it to be. But his veto of British entry into EEC just a few days before the signature of the treaty outraged German politicians of all parties and reminded them of the anti-American implications such a close Franco-German relationship might develop. The Bundestag passed the treaty as a tribute to Adenauer, but they stripped it of its substance by adding a preamble that reaffirmed West Germany's reliance upon the Atlantic alliance as the central pillar of its foreign policy. De Gaulle shrugged off his disappointment: "Treaties are like maidens and roses. They each have their day. . . . 'Hélas, que j'en ai vu mourir de jeunes filles.'"[6] But he pressed on with the least disputed feature of the treaty: the creation of a Franco-German Youth Office that by 1966 had arranged for exchange visits of over a million young people between France and Germany, thus preparing the generation that would begin to move into positions of political power in the 1970s and 1980s for continuing the collaboration. In addition, he began the regular biannual governmental consultations. Neither Chancellor Ludwig Erhard nor Chancellor Kurt-Georg Kiesinger made much effort to revive the momentum of the Franco-German treaty, however, especially as the 1960s were the period when de Gaulle was delivering his most paralyzing blows to the EEC. There was even a certain malice in the manner in which the German newspapers reported the decline of de Gaulle's prestige brought about by the rioting in Paris in May 1968.

Under Pompidou and Giscard d'Estaing, however, a more realistic relationship was achieved, especially as the importance of the United States in European affairs was sapped by the Vietnam war, Watergate, and the economic recession that followed the oil crisis of 1973. Pompidou officially welcomed Brandt's *Ostpolitik* as a breakthrough to the dissipation of tension in Europe that de Gaulle had favored. (At the same time, however, he welcomed Britain into membership with the European Community, partly to satisfy German wishes and partly to offset German strength within the Community.) A more than usually colorful reception for Brandt in Paris in January 1970 seemed to set the seal of French approval on the new German policy toward the east. The harmony was short-lived, however; for Pompidou became increasingly fearful that *Ostpolitik* was leading to the possibility of neutralization in central Europe. For the same reason, Pompidou criticized the Mutual and Balanced Force Reduction Talks (MBFR) between NATO and the Warsaw Pact members, which he felt might lessen France's military security by thinning out the NATO presence in West Germany, and the SALT talks, both of which West Germany was supporting. But the final blow was France's attempt, during the oil crisis of 1973 and 1974, to forge unilaterally a favorable position for itself with the oil producers, while sabotaging—or so it seemed to American and German observers— the attempts of Washington to create a common front for negotiation with OPEC.[7]

Pompidou died in April 1974, and Brandt resigned the following month. Their successors, Valéry Giscard d'Estaing and Helmut Schmidt, were already well acquainted from their work as finance ministers, during which they had, as self-proclaimed pragmatists, quickly developed a close friendship. Both were deeply suspicious of American leadership under Presidents Ford and Carter, and both occasionally expressed their impatience with undiplomatic frankness. Indeed, the double sense of the decline of American power relative to that of the Soviet Union and of the vacillating character of American leadership was the primary factor bringing the two to a harmony of policies. Where in the 1960s de Gaulle had called in vain for a Europe strong enough to resist the overwhelming pressures of the United States, in the 1970s the French and German leaders were recognizing the need to create a Europe strong enough to handle responsibilities that the United States was feared to be too weak to continue. Giscard for example took as the predominant theme of his speeches during his grand tour of West Germany in July 1980 (a tour planned to reenact the dramatic German visit of de Gaulle in 1962) the need for the "two peoples to act together to put an end to the eclipse of Europe." In the main square of Bonn, he declared: "Yesterday we went through the stage of reconciliation. We must undertake now the stage of common action to restore to Europe its role in the affairs of the world."[8]

The main diplomatic instrument for the establishment of common positions by Giscard and Schmidt was the biannual meetings of the heads of government provided for by the Franco-German treaty, of which the Bonn meeting in July 1980 was the thirty-sixth. Both Giscard and Schmidt were usually accompanied by almost all the members of their governments and were thus able to cover the whole gamut of problems concerning the direct relations of the two countries and the policy of the European Community, as well as broader international questions. The meeting of February 1980 was an interesting example of the achievements and the difficulties of this type of negotiation, coming as it did immediately after the invasion of Afghanistan. In addition to the discussion of such European Community matters as the definition of "European judicial territory" for the legal pursuit of terrorist crimes and the working of the European monetary system, they prepared plans for increasing the study of each other's language and for common use of the recently launched French Ariane satellite. But the most significant result of that meeting was their warning to the Russians that the Afghan invasion was unacceptable and that "détente could not resist another shock of the same kind."[9] Although they attempted to put teeth into the declaration by announcing that they were about to begin joint construction of a heavy tank, the final communiqué disappointed most French observers. Like weak parents, declared political scientist Alfred Grosser, they told the Russians, "Be good next time."

In short, the value of the meetings has lain in the specific, bilateral undertakings for which decisions can be implemented. But action on wider issues has been hampered by deep-rooted differences of orientation between the two countries, by fear of arousing the distrust of their partners in the European Community, and by their lack of leverage on the superpowers. In particular, it has been difficult for the Franco-German tandem to influence the Soviets, since the French have been worried about losing their semblance of independence within the Western alliance and the Germans have been disturbed at the possibility of losing the better human contacts developing with East Germany.[10] There has, however, been evidence of a growing willingness on the part of West Germany to pull away from unconditional acceptance of the lead of Washington, as was seen in the communiqué following the meeting of February 1980 when Schmidt and Giscard refused to follow Carter's call for exemplary sanctions against the Russians. "The newest fact in European history," commented Le Nouvel Observateur, "is that the Germans, in the middle of a grave international crisis, instead of aligning themselves unconditionally with Washington, came to Paris to affirm, with their French partner, the existence of specific interests which were not necessarily the same as American interests."[11] It was therefore no surprise that one of Mitterrand's first contacts with a European head of government should have been an amicable meeting with Schmidt in July 1981.

Perhaps more fundamental than the development of the mechanism of common policymaking has been the growth of economic ties between the two countries. France became West Germany's most important customer in 1960. In 1968 it became West Germany's principal supplier. German sales to France rose from 4.9 billion francs in 1960 to 23.4 billion in 1970 and 59.8 billion in 1978. German purchases from France increased from 4.7 billion francs in 1960 to 20.5 billion in 1970 and 70.0 billion in 1978. For the French, these figures implied a growing deficit in trade with Germany due in part to the weakness of the franc in relation to the mark but also due to the extreme difficulty of breaking into the competitive German market for industrial goods. Because of this imbalance the French placed great emphasis on access to the German market for their agricultural goods due to a favorable agricultural policy within the European Community.[12]

French capital investments in West Germany, aided by the freeing of capital flows within the Common Market, totaled $708 million by 1973 and were located primarily in coal, energy, metallurgy, and commercial companies. The most remarkable example was the Saint-Gobain-Pont-à-Mousson company that, with an investment of $149 million in glass and metallurgy, was employing 30,000 German workers. German investment in France, which had remained level with French investment in Germany until 1970, soared in the 1970s and had already reached $1.19 billion by 1973. Cooperation between French and German companies was also far advanced and included the production of the Airbus jet plane and the building of a research reactor for the nuclear energy work of the Franco-German institute of Grenoble. This type of interlocking economy, in which the self-interest of one country is deeply involved in the prosperity of the other, was precisely what Robert Schuman and Jean Monnet had hoped to create when they originally proposed the foundation of the European Coal and Steel Community in 1950. Its existence is the necessary basis for the political collaboration by which France and Germany can lead Europe. As the *Economist* of London wrote in 1979, "The intuitive, joyfully argumentative, nationalist-minded French and the orderly, industrious, cumbersomely sincere Germans make an odd couple. But having embraced each other, they dominate Europe.... France's President Valéry Giscard d'Estaing and Germany's chancellor, Helmut Schmidt, are a two-man band. The rest of Europe marches to their tune."[13]

With no other country did France attempt to achieve so close a relationship, although for a time during the Fourth Republic it appeared that Britain rather than Germany was France's most favored ally. France and Britain concluded the defense treaty of Dunkirk in 1947, and broadened that agreement to include Belgium, the Netherlands, and Luxembourg the next year. The two countries worked closely together to shape the Organization for European Economic Cooperation, and they fought together in the Suez Canal attack in 1956. But as France turned toward the economic integration of Western Europe through the ECSC and EEC, Britain refused closer links to the continent, believing somewhat naively in the strength of its Commonwealth ties and, more realistically, in its special relationship with the United States. De Gaulle made a brief effort to revive the close relationship with Britain when he proposed in 1958 that the Western alliance should be directed by a French-British-American directorate that would draw up strategic plans on a world scale, including rules for the use of nuclear weapons. Rebuffed by both the British and the Americans, he came to regard Britain as little more than America's Trojan Horse and, in the famous press conference of January 14, 1963, dismissed the first British effort to join

EEC on the grounds that the British had not yet become European. For a time in 1971 and 1972, during the negotiations on British entry into the European Community President Pompidou became constructively pro-British, finding the attitudes of British Prime Minister Edward Heath the requisite standard of Europeanism.[14] But the return of the Labour party to power under Harold Wilson (1974–1976) and James Callaghan (1976–1979) reminded the French of the deep-lying distrust of Britain's workers for the European Community, and relations again cooled. Nor was the cordiality revived with the election victory in 1979 of the Conservative party under the leadership of Margaret Thatcher. Thatcher's bellicose stubbornness in forcing a reduction of Britain's financial contribution to the Community—which was successful, although at the price of rousing deep resentment among the other Community members—had the effect of throwing the French and Germans even closer together.

In the late 1970s, however, there were more underlying reasons for the distance between the French and British than conflicts of personality and approach. The French had become convinced, as their own economy surged ahead of that of the British, that Britain had become the sick man of Europe, and hence an ally that might have to be aided rather than relied upon. Even in the five-year period (1973–1977) following Britain's entry into the Community, its GNP (at 1975 prices and exchange rate) rose only from $218.1 billion to $237.9 billion compared to a French growth from $310.2 billion to $365.0 billion. Trade ties were still unsatisfactory, in view of the size of the British population. With 55 million people, Britain purchased 6.5 percent of France's exports and supplied 5.2 percent of its imports. By comparison, the Netherlands, with less than 14 million people, purchased 5.1 percent of French exports and supplied 6.1 percent of its imports.[15] The one great source of strength in the British economy, possession of oil and gas in the North Sea, was not felt to offset Britain's deep-rooted problems of ineffective management and anarchic trade unions; and the French have watched with a mixture of cynicism and good will Thatcher's efforts to purge the British economy with the application of monetarist medicine.

With regard to the countries of southern Europe, France has felt itself a kind of patron, envisaging the establishment of a loose French-led grouping of the Mediterranean powers that would offset in some degree the North European grouping of the British isles, Benelux, and Scandinavia that has regarded Britain as its natural leader. Italy appeared a particularly promising member of such a grouping, with its perennial Christian Democratic leadership and (at least until the late 1960s) its booming economy. But, like Britain, Italy in the 1970s failed to maintain its promise. With the resurgence of terrorism of the Italian Right and Left, and with its unsolved labor problems, its governmental paralysis, and especially the tarnishing of its economic miracle, the French feared for the very survival of a democratic society in Italy. It therefore seemed more promising for France to turn to post-Franco Spain.

Giscard personally attended the coronation of King Juan Carlos in November 1975, a week after the death of Franco, and welcomed the king to Paris the following October. Giscard d'Estaing became the principal supporter of the membership in the European Community not only of Spain but also of Portugal and Greece. France's self-interest, he argued, lay in a rebalancing of the Community between north and south, because France would then become the central region and because, in particular, France would be the necessary linkage between the Iberian peninsula and northern Europe. But Giscard also felt that it was France's vocation to protect the new and still fragile democracies in those three countries whose historic destiny had made them part of European society. "The basic question is this," he told *Le Monde* in 1978. "Must we seek an agreement limited to a few countries? Must we on the contrary organize Europe within the borders of its civilization and its history? Even if in fact that is more difficult, I believe it is the task we must accomplish."[16] Although his enthusiasm for Spanish and Portuguese membership may have weakened between 1979 and 1980 as the Portuguese economy continued to flounder, as the Spanish government seemed ineffective in handling its internal problems of terrorism and economic crisis, and as internal opposition to their European Community membership mounted in France, Giscard d'Estaing remained—in principle at least—the leading proponent of their entry.

What is significant in this attitude toward southern Europe is that there was almost no desire to establish a kind of patron-client relationship in Europe outside the Community. The natural organization within which closer bonds would be created was immediately conceived to be the Community, within which burdens were shared but a position of leadership for France was attainable. In his most important pronouncement on the European Community, a speech given at Hoerdt in

Alsace on May 15, 1979, during the campaign for the election of the European Parliament, Giscard not only justified the integration of the European nation-states but claimed for France a position at their head. Reviving the original motivation for the creation of the ECSC in 1950, he argued that in a world dominated by superpowers of continental size only a united Europe with a population the size of the Soviet Union and an economy the equal of that of the United States could avoid oblivion. "What would our grandchildren in the year 2000 think of us, of you, if they were told that, given this choice, we refused to organize Europe? ... They would think we were blind and cowards." Yet France's subsequent choice was whether to be at the head or the tail of this organization. "We French are not suited to drag up the rear. The genius of France leads it to place itself at the head of those who are defending new and generous ideas. . . . Great Britain, you know, which chose to hamper the construction of Europe, found no advantage in it. Its income twenty years ago was equal to ours. It is 40 percent less today. . . . By being at the head of the European organization, we can orient it toward solutions that conform to our opinions. That is what we have always done."[17]

Giscard, in fact, was attempting to bring off the supreme coup of combining the European concepts of Jean Monnet and Charles de Gaulle to create an integrated community of nations in which leadership would still lie with the individual national governments and not with a supranational Community authority. Analytically, he had gone to the heart of the weakness of both positions. Jean Monnet had wanted to create a United States of Europe, open to all the democratic states of Western Europe and therefore far larger in scale and complexity than the original six-member ECSC. Yet such a union was likely very quickly to lose its cohesion and prove incapable of achieving the supranationalism that it was Monnet's primary aim to achieve. The opening of the European Community to Britain, Ireland, and Denmark had shown that these suspicions were to some degree justified, while the admission of Greece in 1981 (which was likely to be followed in the near future by the admission of Spain and Portugal) was almost certain to dilute the integrationist fervor even more. De Gaulle on the other hand had restricted the Community to the original six, thereby keeping it to a size in which supranationalism might well have been achieved; yet he had at the same time blocked any moves toward a genuine supranationalism.

In order to estimate the viability of an enlarged Community as envisaged by Giscard d'Estaing, it may be helpful to glance back over its evolution from its Monnet-inspired origins to its de Gaulle–modeled transformation in the 1960s. Monnet's original concept, which was accepted
by Foreign Minister Robert Schuman in 1950, was to set in motion the
forces of economic integration by abolishing barriers to the free movement of goods, capital, and workers within the Community in order to
create among the members an economic self-interest in the preservation
of the Community. From this economic self-interest, which would arise
from the stimulus to trade and to production that the enlarged market
would give, would grow the desire for greater political integration. The
Community institutions – an executive Commission, a European Parliament, and a Court of Justice – would exist as the nucleus for a future
political government to which ever larger powers could be entrusted,
thereby bringing into being in gradual stages a United States of Europe.
In the 1950s, when the European states were painfully rebuilding their
economies and remained deeply aware of their relative insigificance in
comparison with the superpowers, these ideas were appealing. Economic
success did follow creation of the ECSC and EEC. The ECSC stimulated coal and steel production to such a degree that it even became necessary to phase out coal production in the more out-of-date regions of
the ECSC and to moderate the excessive outpouring of steel. The lesson
of the early years of the ECSC was quickly interpreted by the integra-
tionists to imply that only total integration, rather than integration
restricted to two sectors of the economy, could enable the Community
to achieve its full potential. The Treaty of Rome (1957), creating the
European Economic Community, therefore provided for the inclusion
of both industry and agriculture and for the eventual conversion of the
Community into a full economic union. The successes of the EEC were
outstanding from its creation in 1958 until the oil crisis of 1973. As we
saw in Chapter 2, these years were a period of growth and prosperity
unparalleled in French history. It was not only the existence of the EEC
that stimulated this progress. Population growth, government planning,
restructuring of agriculture, massive investments to increase industrial
productivity, even a change in entrepreneurial attitudes – all had contributed to the boom. It has also become evident since 1973 that under-
appreciated contributions were also being made by cheap and abundant
supplies of oil and by low-priced raw materials from the Third World.

Yet the vital role of the EEC was proven by the much faster rate of growth of French trade with its EEC partners than with any other part of the world. In 1959, only 16 percent of French exports was sent to its five EEC partners; in 1977, 42.7 percent was sold to them. In 1959, those five partners supplied 26.7 percent of French imports; by 1977, that figure had risen to 43.2 percent.[18] And, as in the case of Germany, an interlocking structure of investments, partnerships, subsidiaries, patents, and so on had arisen to make integration a reality of the daily economic life of the Community.

Yet almost nothing had been done to advance the Community toward the political integration Monnet had thought would arise naturally from this economic integration. De Gaulle and the Gaullists are often blamed for interrupting the evolution from economic to political integration. De Gaulle was the most vituperative of the opponents of supranationalism, with his taunts at the faceless technocrats of Brussels, his evocation of the glories of nationalism in comparison with the ignominy of a civilization of Esperanto or Volapük, and with his warnings of the danger of a so-called supranational Europe being lost in a colossal Atlantic community. He also took specific steps to halt the move to political integration, most notably in the "empty chair crisis" of 1966–1967 by which he compelled the Community to abandon the move to majority voting in the Council of Ministers and thus to leave France with veto power. Yet it must also be remembered that de Gaulle was instrumental in compelling France's partners to create a common agricultural policy (CAP), permitting Community preference against outside producers, and establishing Community-wide agricultural prices. The weaknesses of such a policy are evident, especially to the industrial countries that must pay prices that are often two or three times the world level. But, without the existence of a Community policy for agriculture, the Community would have been unworkably tilted toward the major industrial powers. De Gaulle also, by his two vetoes (of 1963 and 1967) on British membership, kept the Community at a size large enough for economic integration to be effective. Whether de Gaulle was in fact preparing the way for political integration in the future is questionable, although, as Giscard d'Estaing reminded his audience at Hoerdt, de Gaulle had told his cabinet in 1961: "This Europe will have to be built one day. It has been discussed since Julius Caesar, Charlemagne, Otto, Charles V, Louis XIV, Napoleon, Hitler. That Europe, I shall not see it myself but you"—turning to Giscard d'Estaing, then a young state secretary—"you will see it."[19]

Pompidou edged slowly away from de Gaulle's intransigence. His decision to agree to the admission of Britain to the Community was a calculated risk based on his belief that Britain had been compelled to give enough guarantees of its conversion to Europeanism to be admitted. Britain's demand in 1974 for a renegotiation of its terms of entry was therefore a bitter disappointment for him, as it seemed to cast doubt upon the possible success of his other moves to give the Community a "confederal" character. Pompidou believed in summitry more at the Community than at the world level, and he was primarily responsible for calling the three meetings of the Community heads of government—at The Hague (December 1969), in Paris (October 1972), and in Copenhagen (December 1973). The Paris summit was responsible for the agreement to proceed to create the vaguely defined economic union by 1980, a plan that was later dropped partly for its own lack of clarity and partly because of the energy crisis and the subsequent European recession.

Giscard attempted to go further toward the construction of a European confederation. Before becoming president, he had personally represented his political party, the Independent Republicans, in Monnet's Action Committee for the United States of Europe and had developed close personal friendship with Monnet, who supported Giscard's presidential candidacy in 1974. As president, he immediately declared that he saw the need to end the veto power France had retained after the empty-chair crisis, although what he proposed to substitute was rather vague. He called a fourth summit meeting of the heads of government of the Community in Paris in December 1974, and persuaded the members to agree to meet in a "European Council" three times every year. In return, he agreed in principle to the election of the European Parliament by universal suffrage (which finally took place in 1979), thereby enhancing the prestige and possibly the power of that body. And he accepted the formation of a European Regional Development Fund, which would primarily benefit Britain and Italy. From these moves he envisaged the emergence of a European confederation of states that would be his own grand design: "The European confederation will have an original structure with three branches: an executive branch formed from the European Council, an administrative branch for Community matters derived from the Commission, and a branch with a deliberative and legislative function for Community questions derived from the Assembly."[20] Thus, Community institutions would retain their functions, while the will of the individual states would be expressed through the European Council. The European Council, in fact, would be the principal institution within the confederation, and the success of its evolution would condition the nature of the confederation. In its first six years of activity the Council proved very effective in permitting the Community not only to advance its economic integration but also to develop common stances in relation to the rest of the world. The European Monetary System, formulated at the three European Council meetings in 1978, is an example of the former. Backed largely by France and West Germany, the system provided for the close alignment of the value of the currencies of members, pooling of reserves in order to back currencies falling below the assigned limits, and establishment of a reserve facility known as the European Currency Unit (ECU). (Britain, however, refused to join the European Monetary System because of the weakness of its currency.) The most important example of coordination on foreign policy matters was the Community's presentation of a common position at the Helsinki security conference. Thus, by the beginning of the 1980s, the Community seemed to be moving successfully toward a workable confederal system, although it remained very doubtful whether France's partners would cede France the kind of leadership role Giscard claimed its merits deserved.[21]

It is thus important for the United States to appreciate that the role of France in Western Europe has evolved considerably since the presidency of de Gaulle, and it is still evolving. In the first place, Franco-German partnership has become a constant in European politics and diplomacy and will certainly continue to be so regardless of change of personalities. The solidity of the reconciliation, with its basis in economic self-interest as well as psychological rapprochement, gives it its ongoing character and its position as one of the bases of Western strength. Indeed, it is the relationship with West Germany that is perhaps most instrumental in bringing France into the Western alliance. While at times, most obviously at the Western economic summits, this relationship may have appeared to have anti-American implications, its value is fundamental to the successful maintenance of an Atlantic community. Second, the part of France in holding together the countries of Mediterranean Europe and in linking the democracies of northern and southern Europe is of considerable significance. The French, as we shall see in Chapter 8, have had considerable experience – and difficulty – in reconciling the north and south of their own country; and it is possible that from this experience they bring more idealism and more realism to the task of harmonizing the north and south of Europe than a purely northern or a purely southern power could. Since the restoration of democracy in Spain, Portugal, and Greece has been one of the most positive features in the evolution of the West in the 1970s, it is vital to support that evolution, which France has done. All three countries face the danger of geographical isolation as well as the problems of economic underdevelopment, and French moves to bring them into the European Community – moves that are especially laudable since their products will compete directly with France's own Mediterranean products – need all possible support. Third, the French concept of a European confederation, coming as a midway solution between what was proving to be an unrealizable concept of total integration and a dangerously realizable reversion into total disintegration, offers considerable hope for a slow but solid formation of a political community in Western Europe. Whenever possible, it thus becomes desirable to negotiate with the European Community as a whole, in order to reinforce the political will of the Community and to encourage the experience, in a confederal form, of a political union.

To what extent is the community of interest and sympathy that has grown up between the United States and France in the years since the Second World War similar in character to that formed between France and West Germany? At first sight, it would appear that this question is only too easy to answer. A majority of the French still regard the Americans as imperialists like the Russians. In 1980, 51 percent of those questioned in a public opinion poll agreed that it was correct to accuse the Americans of imperialism, and only 33 percent disagreed.[22] Numerous books have been published to show the French the form this imperialism has taken in France. Multinational companies have been shown to be taking over the French economy. American monetary policy, which caused high interest rates in the United States and resulted in a surge in the value of the dollar, was held responsible for the international financial disorder of the late 1970s and early 1980s and thus for the problems of the franc and in part for the recession in France. In 1980, in a blistering study called *France Colonized*, Jacques Thibau repeated a widely held

French belief that American cultural influences had followed the economic penetration, changing French taste in music, literature, art, and even clothing.[23] The Americanization of France had even attacked that most sacred repository of the French national spirit, the language, making it necessary for the French government to attempt to ban the use of "Franglais" and "Galloricains." As Alfred Grosser has pointed out, "the dominating tendency in France when faced by the United States is to compensate for a feeling of economic inferiority by a feeling of cultural superiority, which has heavy political consequences."[24] The Americans for their part have responded with the accusation that France has been a spoiler in European and at times even in world affairs.[25] From the major disappointments of the presidency of de Gaulle to the minor irritations of the presidency of Giscard d'Estaing, France has not received a good press in the United States.[26]

Yet, as this book has attempted to show, the outlook for relations between the two countries is basically optimistic. Economically, the two countries are continually growing closer. In spite of the various monetary crises, trade expanded rapidly throughout the 1970s. Between 1974 and 1978 alone, American exports to France doubled in value, and French exports to the United States increased by one-third. But the possibilities for the future are even greater since the extent of trade between the two countries is small in relation to the size of the two national markets. Cultural exchanges, traditionally a bond between the two countries since the eighteenth century, have remained strong. Perhaps no country in Europe is so closely aware of trends in the American artistic world as France. In fact, it is probably true that American writers, artists, and musicians are better known in France than French cultural leaders are known in the United States. Educational exchanges, which became frequent after the Second World War, have also remained significant, although they have not reached the level of American exchanges with such countries as West Germany or Britain.[27] Militarily, in spite of the fact that the French military forces do not participate in NATO, there has been continuing consultation within the planning groups of that organization. And, as was seen in Chapter 3, French forces remain an important part of Western defenses in the eventuality of a conflict with the Soviet bloc. Finally, political cooperation has continued in spite of periods of bickering and recrimination, although the most fruitful contacts have probably been those within multilateral settings such as the economic summit meeting at Venice in 1980.

With the exception of the Communists and the small extreme-left groups, all political parties in France recognize the value of this tiered alliance system. Thus, although there may be changes of emphasis in the near future, the United States can expect France to continue to follow an alliance policy that is basically in harmony with U.S. goals.

8

The Challenges
to National Unity

The irony of France's assumption of the role of spokesman for the European nation-state is that, of all the European nations, France is one of those most threatened by deep internal divisions. These divisions are of many kinds. National minorities (i.e., those minorities incorporated into the French state during the historic process of unification, not those minorities, such as the Algerians, who have come to France by immigration) challenge the very supremacy of the "French" within the boundaries of the present French state. In west and southwest France deep resentment is felt at the long-standing gap in economic well-being between those parts of the country and the more affluent north and east—a disparity for which the excessive concentration of wealth and talent in Paris and the surrounding region is seen to be largely responsible. The unequal distribution of economic opportunity and of reward within French society has produced a cleavage down the very center of the French class structure: almost half of the population is in search of a deep-rooted transformation of their society, while most of the other half is determined to hold on to the privileges three decades of economic growth have made increasingly attractive. Finally, internal economic and social divisions have produced a polarized political system that is exemplified by the presidential election of 1974 in which victor Valéry Giscard d'Estaing received only 1.6 percent more of the vote than his challenger, François Mitterrand. For this present study, the overall question that arises from consideration of France's internal divisions is whether, either singly or in combination, those divisions are likely in the future to change French policy, either nationally or internationally. Or, to put the matter in a different way, are the internal cleavages in French society so great that the vaunted *France une et indivisible* can have only a limited future?

The demands of French regional national minorities for greater recognition and rights within France have existed for centuries, but only in the past two decades have they been so widely publicized—partly due to the violence of terrorist groups and partly, and more significantly, due to widespread public support within the minority region.[1] The most restrictive definition of the national minorities within France is those who speak a regional language. Although precise statistics do not exist, it is estimated that 5 million French people speak a regional language daily, while another 10 million speak one on occasion. However, these estimates include the undoubtedly inflated figures of 2 million who daily speak a variety of Occitanian, which comprises the dialects south of the Loire, such as Gascon, Provençal, or Auvergnat, and another 8 million who speak it occasionally. More insistent on recognition are the 700,000 people who speak Breton, the 1.5 million Alsatians who speak German, the 150,000 Corsicans who speak Corsican, the 100,000 Basques in southwest France who speak the Basque language, the 200,000 people in Roussillon who speak Catalan, and the 80,000 people in the Nord who speak Flemish. All of these groups have been demanding the teaching of their language and literature in the schools and universities, their own television programs, and so on.[2] The problem becomes broader, however, when one includes all those who speak French but feel themselves to be members of a minority by virtue of their national origins. There are, for example about 3 million Bretons in Brittany and about 270,000 Corsicans in Corsica, while many more people with one or more Breton or Corsican parents or grandparents live in other parts of France. These are sizable numbers, and the French state has very slowly and reluctantly begun to grant some of their cultural demands.

A sense of frustration with French administration and a feeling of exploitation has, however, led small numbers of the more extreme activists to turn to terrorism in support of their demands for political autonomy, while others, more numerous, have turned to political activity to win concessions that would vary from greater educational programs, such as the foundation of a University in Corsica, to greater political control of their own regions. The most active of the terrorist groups have been Breton, and some of their members may have had ties with the Irish Republican Army in Ireland. Their activities have included bombings of power stations and security forces' vehicles as well as the bombing of one hall of the Palace of Versailles. The National Liberation Front of Corsica has also used bombings against targets representing mainland capital or the governmental machinery of Paris. The government has proceeded strongly against these activists, banning their organizations and arresting some of their leaders. Nevertheless a network of terrorists still exists in Brittany and Corsica, and especially in Corsica, that network remains a constant intrusion on the smooth functioning of daily life. It seems likely that the work of the terrorists has been counterproductive, and that they have lost the support of even those who had originally applauded their efforts, especially where the terrorists have shifted from actions against public property to attacks on people. It is thus doubtful whether these small groups can achieve the kind of disruption of society that is being achieved by right- and left-wing terrorists in Italy and by the Basques in Spain.[3]

In the past 30 years the massive programs of the French government to bridge the gap in living standards between the underdeveloped west and southwest of France and the rest of the country have diluted the appeal of separatism or of autonomy to the regional minorities. The cultural grievances of national minorities were more pressing when they were combined with the knowledge that their regions were also economically deprived in comparison with "French France." The publication in 1947 of Jean-François Gravier's *Paris and the French Desert* brought widespread recognition of the extraordinary disparities that existed between developed and underdeveloped France, and the first regional statistics developed by the French government upheld Gravier's accusations. In the mid-1950s, regional income per capita in the Paris region was almost exactly twice that of the poorer regions of the country (Corsica, Limousin, Midi-Pyrénées, and Brittany), even when transfer payments from social security were taken into account. Moreover, every other statistic — unemployment, out-migration, ownership of tractors, availability of medical care, standards of housing, and so on — repeated the same basic inequality. Fortunately, the French government realized in time the deep anger roused in the underprivileged areas of the country, especially at a period when the French economy as a whole was beginning to boom. A national program of regional development was begun in 1950 and has become increasingly ambitious.

The local administrative structure was reshaped, with the grouping of departments into 22 larger regions (often corresponding to the old provinces such as Burgundy or Languedoc) within which development programs could be planned. Massive financial aid was made available for restructuring agriculture and to encourage movement of industry into the underdeveloped regions of the west and south. New organizations, often combining governmental and private resources, were created to undertake vast economic projects (e.g., the creation of a tourist industry on the Languedoc coast and the irrigation of farmland in eastern Corsica). In 1972, new representative bodies, a Regional Council and an Economic and Social Council, were set up in each region to provide local participation in the development programs. Although progress has been painfully slow, largely because of the deeply ingrained character of the sociological and economic difficulties faced, these programs have begun to show results. Although there was disappointment at the small degree to which the disparities between regions were overcome, and especially at the failure to reduce the gap between the Paris region and the rest, the poorer regions achieved an absolute increase in economic well-being to which the industrial and agricultural programs made an important contribution. In regions like Corsica, there was a reversal of migration trends, the return of former migrants indicating clearly that higher standards of life and of economic opportunity had been achieved. Moreover, through their regional bodies, the people of the poorer areas were finding a means of expressing their wishes and their discontents, which they had felt inadequately provided for in the Parisian assemblies. Thus, it is probably fair to say that the imaginative programs of regional development implemented by the French government, in spite of their shortcomings, have had a beneficial effect in moderating the division within France due to the uneven geographic distribution of wealth. They have diminished the discontent and especially the sense of frustration that in the early 1950s had provided a certain legitimacy to the demands of the regional autonomists.

However, even more serious regional problems faced the French in the remaining parts of their empire. On the Caribbean island of Guadeloupe the systematic bombing by the Group of Armed Liberation of various buildings regarded as symbols of French authority culminated in the explosion of a large dynamite charge at the airport just before the arrival in January 1981 of Giscard d'Estaing, and served as a reminder that these regional problems must be dealt with.

Since the independence of the Comores in 1975, Djibouti in 1977, and the New Hebrides in 1980, France's remaining overseas possessions have consisted of five Overseas Departments, three Overseas Territories, and a "territorial collectivity" (Mayotte) with a special status. The departments include two Caribbean islands (Guadeloupe and Martinique), Guyana on the north coast of South America, the two tiny islands jointly known as Saint-Pierre-and-Miquelon off the coast of Newfoundland, and the island of Réunion in the Indian Ocean. Three of the territories are in the South Pacific; they are French Polynesia (of which Tahiti is the center), Wallis and Futuna, and New-Caledonia. Mayotte is in the Indian Ocean. Table 8.1 indicates their size and economic significance to France.

The islands obviously have strategic importance for France, however small they may be. Réunion and Mayotte are well located in the Indian Ocean. New-Caledonia and Polynesia maintain French presence in the South Pacific and are especially important since the granting of independence to Vanuatu (New Hebrides) in 1980 by Britain and France who had governed the islands jointly since 1888. Guyana is the site of the Kourou rocket-launching center and Polynesia the site of a much-criticized nuclear experimental station. New-Caledonia is important for its rich resources in nickel, cobalt, iron, manganese, and silver. Unfortunately, the more delightful of the islands became a final refuge for many French people abandoning other colonies that had received their independence. Race relations on Guadeloupe, for example, soured between 1975 and 1980 because of a large influx of French settlers from Djibouti. But throughout the islands there has been a sense of grievance at French rule. In Polynesia, it was due above all to the persistence of

TABLE 8.1

OVERSEAS DEPARTMENTS AND TERRITORIES OF FRANCE

	Population (in thousands)	Density (inhab./sq. km.)	G.N.P. (millions of francs)	Principal Resources
DEPARTMENTS				
Guadeloupe	325 (1974)	182 (1974)	3888 (1977)	Sugar, rum, bananas, tourism
Martinique	325 (1974)	295 (1974)	5265 (1977)	Sugar, rum, bananas, pineapples, tourism
Guyana	55 (1974)	1 (1974)	na	Wood, shrimp, Kourou space center
Saint-Pierre-and-Miquelon	6 (1974)	25 (1974)	na	Beef, fish
Réunion	477 (1974)	190 (1974)	6837 (1977)	Sugar cane, perfume, rum
TERRITORIES				
French Polynesia	137 (1977)	34 (1977)	2845 (1976)	Copra, tourism, nuclear experiment station
New-Caledonia	133 (1976)	7 (1976)	3495 (1976)	Nickel, chrome
Wallis and Futuna	9 (1976)	36 (1976)		
Mayotte*	47 (1978)	126 (1978)		Naval base

SOURCE: INSEE, Tableaux de l'économie française, 1980, p. 11
* Mayotte has a special status intermediary between department and territory.

the French in continuing their atomic testing. In Réunion and Mayotte, the desire for independence was encouraged by the Organization of African Unity. In New-Caledonia, the development of mineral resources was felt by some to be a continuance of colonial exploitation for the primary benefit of French investors. Demands for change varied from the desire for greater government investment in education and infrastructure to desire for outright independence. Opposition to French rule was equally varied. On Saint-Pierre-and-Miquelon it led to a general strike in March 1980, which was only ended when gendarmes were flown in to help the local police. In Guadeloupe and Martinique, Europeans were threatened directly, while the liberation groups emulated the Corsicans and Bretons in their bombing campaigns and Cuba openly backed their demands for independence. Thus, while in the 1980s there seems to be a good prospect that economic development will calm the demands of the regional minorities within France, it seems that the Overseas Departments and Territories might well explode into violence, not least because of the interest of such foreign powers as Cuba in their future evolution.

Much less progress has been made in solving the problem of the deep inequalities within French society in distribution of wealth and income, and in access to training and careers that merit the higher incomes. There is a fairly widespread belief in France that inequality there is greater than in the other industrialized countries of the West; the existence of this belief undoubtedly adds to the social tension. In reality, the inequalities in France are approximately the same as those in West Germany or Belgium, and notably less than those still existing in Britain. Nevertheless, they are sufficiently great to be a cause of tension.

The French statistical office INSEE and the *Centre d'Etudes des Revenus et des Coûts* (CERC) have recently established for 1975 the first reliable study of distribution of wealth within French society.[4] Total wealth in the hands of private individuals (excluding retirement and insurance benefits and certain unverifiable personal possessions such as jewelry and gold) was estimated to be 4800 billion francs ($1090 billion). INSEE and CERC set out to find the relationship between income received by the different percentiles of the French population and total wealth possessed. Their findings are summarized in Table 8.2. The figures were calculated for the 22.5 million people who filed tax returns.

Table 8.2 shows that the 20 percent of the population with the lowest income possessed 6.6 percent of the wealth. When expressed in socio-professional groupings, the disparity becomes even more marked. The average wealth of workers, agricultural laborers, and service personnel was 81,300 francs ($18,477) compared to an average of 1,322,300 francs ($300,522) possessed by approximately one quarter of a million industrialists and business people or the average of 1,334,500 francs ($305,568) of the 170,000 employed in the professions (e.g., doctors and lawyers).

However, when the individuals were grouped solely by percentage of wealth possessed, as was done in a study in 1977 by the *Centre d'Etude de l'Epargne*, the differences are staggering. The lowest 30 percent of the population possessed only 1 percent of the wealth. The top 20 percent possessed 69 percent of the wealth, the top 5 percent possessed 45 percent, and the top 1 percent possessed 26 percent. Moreover, the disparity in wealth had been growing in the boom years up to 1963, as both land and stocks and bonds increased rapidly in value. Since 1963, the distribution of wealth has apparently remained stable. These figures do

TABLE 8.2

WEALTH OF INCOME GROUPS IN FRENCH POPULATION, 1975

Income Group (percentiles)	Average Wealth (francs)	Share of Wealth (percentage)
1–20	70,450	6.6
21–30	124,650	5.8
31–40	135,900	6.4
41–50	137,700	6.5
51–60	146,800	6.9
61–70	179,350	8.4
71–80	211,100	9.9
81–90	292,650	13.7
91–95	434,300	10.2
96–98	692,800	9.8
99	1,031,500	4.8
100	2,354,550	11.0

SOURCE: Philippe Madinier and Jean-Jacques Malpot, "La Répartition du patrimoine des particuliers," *Economie et Statistique*, No. 114 (September 1979), p. 87.

not make the upper 1 percent of the French population unique among the Western countries. The comparable figure for the United States was 27–24 percent possessed by the upper one percent in the 1950s and 1960s, while the share of the upper one percent in Britain was still 30 percent in 1970.[5]

Differences in income paid to the different groups in French society have been an even more burning issue than the differences in wealth. The sense of injustice widely felt in France at the inequality of the distribution of income between different groups of society led the government to form a special commission in preparation of the Seventh Economic and Social Development Plan for 1976–1980, called the Commission on Social Inequalities. The commission found that inequalities existed throughout the economy. One of the most notable was between salaries paid for different economic activities, with the lowest salaries being paid in agriculture and related trades, such as the lumber industry, and in industries employing large numbers of women, such as the textile industry. Whereas in 1974 the average salary in banking was $7,425, the average salary in the textile industry was $4,706 and in nursing and domestic services only $3,468. The spread between salaries paid by type of work and skill was perhaps even more important. Whereas the average pay for male manual laborers was $3,487, for middle-level administrators it was $8,964, and for upper-level administrators $18,056. These inequalities were growing slowly during the postwar period—at least until 1960—but have fallen slowly since. Perhaps the most shocking fact revealed in the 1974 survey was that one-third of the employed work force received less than 15,000 francs ($3,177), the minimum wage being established at $1.29 per hour.[6] (By 1978, it had been raised to $2.29.)

The inability of the mass of the population to advance through education or work experience into the higher paid strata of society was also an embittering factor. In 1974, only 12 percent of students enrolled in higher education were the children of workers, although this percentage was an improvement from the mere 5 percent of 1960. At the summit, the situation was even worse. The very top level of French government and business was a Parisian oligarchy, as Alain Peyrefitte remarks in his scathing indictment of French society, Le Mal français, recruited in large part from a restricted social group resident in a small area of the capital. The children of this elite dominated entrance to the famous grandes *écoles*, the small number of prestigious colleges specializing mainly in engineering, applied science, and administration that train the majority of France's leading government and private administrators and engineers. Although attempts have been made to democratize entry into the *grandes écoles*, by, for example, reserving half the places at the National School of Administration for students from the provinces and from poorer families, Peyrefitte held in 1976 that discrimination was still applied against the new recruits in later assignments.[7] This ruling elite, "who speak the same language, use the same abbreviations, affect the same vocal intonations, who understand each other by inflexion," formed an establishment whose ties spread through politics, bureaucracy, medicine, scientific research, the universities, and the press.

The student riots and the workers' strikes of 1968 illustrated the grievances that these inequalities and blockages in French society have nurtured.[8] The students had a variety of political causes — protest against American involvement in Vietnam, anger at the authoritarian rule of de Gaulle, and distrust of capitalist society in general and fury at the conditions of life in the outer slums of Paris in particular. But what united the majority was a sense of frustration with the university for its outmoded curriculum, indifferent professors, out-of-date rules, and irrelevance to what they perceived as the real problems of economic and social life. All of these shortcomings they blamed on the French state. Although the strikes and factory seizures that followed the student demonstrations were often led by younger workers who saw the union leaders as accomplices of an exploitative economic system, the majority of workers were eventually pacified by specifically economic gains including a wage increase, shortening of the work week, and earlier retirement. What was clear was that the grievances of both students and workers were so deeply felt and so widespread that they could bring about temporary paralysis of their society and, it seemed for a time, could even threaten overthrow of the government. But it was also evident that only a minority of workers and students wished totally to remodel their form of society and government by revolutionary action. It was sufficient for the government to make material concessions to both groups and to allow the inconvenience of the disorders to be widely felt for the wave of protest to lose its strength. The resentment remained, but the sense that the evolution of French society could be changed by direct action had faded. The search for a remedy to injustice was once again channeled back into the established political system, and this system has not worked well in providing those remedies.

The constitution of the Fifth Republic established a sharp division of powers between the legislature and the executive, slanting the balance toward the executive. The constitution sought in particular to end those characteristics of the legislature the Gaullists felt had weakened the Fourth Republic, notably the proliferation of parties, the frequent over-throw of governments, the alternation in power of members of the legis-lature, and the excessive sphere of action of the legislature. First, election to the National Assembly was through single-member constitu-encies, by two-ballot voting. A candidate who achieved on the first ballot 51 percent of the votes cast and one-quarter of the voters regis-tered was elected. On a second ballot, a plain majority sufficed. In effect, most elections were decided on the second ballot as a result of the with-drawal (by mutual bargaining among the parties) of the majority of the candidates. In theory, this system weeded out parties that were unable to form working alliances with others, and thus encouraged compromise and moderation. Second, the legislature was permitted to overthrow the premier and his government only in votes on strictly defined issues of general policy, in votes of censure, or in no-confidence votes. The number of occasions when such a vote was possible was severely re-stricted. Third, if a member of the legislature was appointed a member of the cabinet, he or she had to resign from the parliament. Fourth, and perhaps most important, clauses 34–38 of the constitution defined very narrowly the powers of the legislature and assigned all other powers to the executive, including even the power (with the consent of the legis-lature) to take over during times of crisis the powers assigned to the legislature.

Thus, while the legislature is theoretically the constitutional organ in which all sections of French society should feel themselves to be repre-sented and in which the demands for reform can be formulated in an ef-fective manner, it is doubtful whether the system has worked that way. Perhaps the most central issue of all is whether the political system of the Fifth Republic has produced a grouping of the French parties into two currents of opinion—organized by consultation among themselves —that can present to the French electorate a coherent choice by nomination of their own candidates at the time of the presidential elections of candidates. What has occurred, in fact, is that neither the parties on the left nor the parties on the right have been able to form a consensus. But since the Right, until 1981, had been closer to a consensus than the Left (and was the inheritor of what remained of the de Gaulle mystique), it usually had a slight edge over its opposition in the election campaigns. In 1981, the Right's inability to unite against Socialist candidate Mitterrand contributed greatly to his victory.

The vote for the Communists in parliamentary elections remained remarkably stable during the Fifth Republic, even during the crisis following the events of May 1968: 18.9 percent in 1958, 21.8 percent in 1962, 22.5 percent in 1967, 20.3 percent in 1968, 21.3 percent in 1973, 20.6 percent in 1978, but only 16 percent in 1981. Backed by the 2.4-million-member *Confédération Générale du Travail*, the Communist party found its basic support among urban workers, agricultural labor, and an influential segment of the intellectuals. Its remarkable capacity to survive had been shown in its revival after the two waves of defections that followed Khrushchev's de-Stalinization speech at the twentieth Party congress in 1956 and the Soviet invasion of Czechoslovakia in 1968. One stratagem in its search for respectability was its cautious pulling away from the Soviet line in foreign policy and its reconciliation with the Socialist party. As early as 1964, the Communists had made a major break with their earlier policy by recognizing the justification of a plurality of parties, although it was uncertain whether this change of heart was by conviction or for electoral gain. In 1966 they disapproved the Soviet condemnation of writers Siniavaski and Daniel, and in 1968 they criticized the invasion of Czechoslovakia. That year they also drew up with the Socialists a Common Declaration that was expanded in 1972 to become a Joint Program on which the two parties ran their election campaigns for the next two years. In 1975, French Communist party leader Marchais even seemed to side openly with the Eurocommunists by issuing a joint declaration with Italian Party leader Enrico Berlinguer, whose independent line was bringing him increasingly into trouble with the Soviet leadership. But these initiatives of the French Communists proved to be transitory. The results of the 1973 and 1974 elections appeared to show that the principal gainer from a Communist-Socialist alliance was the Socialists and that the Communist party would have to take a subordinate role in any coalition government resulting from a victory in either the legislative or presidential election.

The showdown for the alliance with the Socialists proved to be the parliamentary elections of 1978 that, according to the polls, seemed likely to be won by the Communist-Socialist alliance. Throughout the election campaign, Marchais systematically undercut his ally Socialist François Mitterrand and at one time even called him a liar. As one commentator noted, even though they hastily compromised between the first and second ballots, they managed, as a result of their bickering, to snatch defeat out of the jaws of victory.

Clearly, this situation presented the greatest tactical problem for the Socialist party. During the Fourth Republic, under the leadership of Guy Mollet, the Socialists were unable to find a natural constituency among the French electorate because their reformism and their willingness to work with the free enterprise system alienated them from many workers. During the Fifth Republic, under Mitterrand's leadership, the party increased its base of support by winning over many of the advancing elements in French society—e.g., the younger technicians, civil servants, and the liberal professions. It also dropped its traditional anticlericalism and opened itself to committed Catholics, who now form one-third of its activists. Its problem in national elections was clear: Too close an alliance with the Communists would drive away many of its own supporters on the right; without the Communists, it was doubtful it could win elections. But during and after the 1978 elections a possibility was emerging. For the party in national elections and for its candidate Mitterrand in the presidential election, it was possible that, by keeping the Communists at a distance, reform-minded voters would be won over from the governmental majority. (However this strategy was challenged within the Socialist party, by its own left wing.) Finally, a further complicating factor on the left was the activity of a number of extreme left-wing groups (such as the *Ligue Communiste Révolutionnaire*), who together received 3.3 percent of the vote in 1978 and of environmentalists, who won 2.14 percent for their antinuclear, antiurban program.

The broad governmental grouping on the right was thus able, through 1980, to profit from the divisions within the opposition, but it was itself fragmented. The so-called center, whose constantly shifting groups sometimes ally with the government and sometimes oppose it, is the most conspicuous example of the continuation of the party feuding of the Fourth Republic—perhaps because its groups are direct descendants of the Radicals and the Christian-Democratic M.R.P. of that Republic. The leaders' personalities play a large part in the shifts of these centrist groups. For example, Jean-Jacques Servan-Schreiber, the dynamic Radical leader, was made minister of reforms in Giscard's first cabinet in 1974, only to be fired a few months later for publicly criticizing continued nuclear testing. Christian Democratic leader Jean Lecanuet oscillated between Giscard and the opposition. In 1978, however, just one month before the parliamentary elections, the Radicals and Lecanuet's newly named *Centre des Démocrates Sociaux* joined in an electoral coalition with Giscard d'Estaing's Independent Republicans, forming the *Union pour la Démocratie Française* (UDF). The essential core of this grouping was the Independent Republicans (renamed *Parti Républicain* in 1977), a party that has to a large extent been the creation of Giscard d'Estaing himself. Staking out a position slightly to the left of the Gaullists, the party stood for encouragement of business, increased social reforms, and a more cooperative attitude toward European integration. Its greatest asset was the popularity the young Giscard d'Estaing had acquired as a brilliant finance minister under de Gaulle and Pompidou—the popularity that enabled him to defeat the Gaullist candidate Jacques Chaban-Delmas in the first round of voting in the presidential election of 1974 and thus to win the support of a united Right to defeat the Socialist Mitterrand in the second round of ballotting. With the patronage and prestige of the presidency, Giscard d'Estaing was able to increase the party's support to the point that, with its partners in the UDF, it finally received greater voter support than the Gaullists in the elections to the European Parliament in 1979.

The Gaullist party was renamed several times in efforts to give it a new image. The original *Union pour la Nouvelle République* (UNR) of 1958 was renamed *Union des Démocrates pour la République* (UDR) in 1974 but proved ineffective in pushing its orthodox Gaullist candidate Chaban-Delmas against Giscard d'Estaing for the presidency. Giscard's first premier, the brilliant but prickly Jacques Chirac, was chosen to give the president the backing of the UDR, but the personalities of the two proved incompatible. Complaining that Giscard was monarchical and that he denied the premier the powers necessary to carry out his job, Chirac resigned in 1976 and turned to the renovation of the Gaullist party, which was renamed the *Rassemblement pour la République* (RPR) in December 1976. The following year, Chirac gained an independent base of electoral strength by winning election as mayor of Paris. Using this position and his leadership of the RPR, he embarked upon a campaign to present himself as an alternative candidate to Giscard in the next presidential elections. To complicate matters further within the Gaullist party, several other long-time Gaullists with impeccable credentials jockeyed for power—especially the three former premiers Michel Debré, Jacques Chaban-Delmas, and Pierre Messmer.

It was partly to free himself from these battles among political personalities that Giscard chose as successor to Chirac the highly respected economist Raymond Barre. Barre received the unenviable task of imposing economic austerity programs and shouldering (in place of the president) the consequent public unpopularity. But the battle for personal power within the right was not assuaged by this tactic; and thus, if the Left was sharply divided among its groups on political principle, the Right remained divided, although less decisively, by struggles of personality.

As a result of this seemingly interminable infighting at a time when they perceived their personal well-being to be constantly deteriorating, the French public became disenchanted. In a poll in November 1980, 80 percent of those questioned said that the current political debate did not interest them because important problems were not discussed.[9] Yet the French remained deeply concerned with the political process. In the 1978 elections, the amazing turnout of eligible voters was 83 percent on the first ballot and 85 percent on the second. This compares very favorably with the 53 percent turnout in the United States in the 1980 presidential election. Yet the result of that election, as of the 1974 presidential election, was to demonstrate the division of France into two voting blocs of almost equal strength. On the second ballot in 1978, the governmental parties took 50.7 percent of the vote, and the opposition 49.3 percent. In 1974, on the second ballot, Giscard received 50.8 percent of the vote, Mitterrand 49.2 percent. Thus the smallest shift of public opinion could swing the vote away from the parties that had held power in France since 1958.[10]

The first round of voting in the 1981 presidential election indicated that just such a shift was under way. Giscard's margin over Mitterrand (28 percent to 25 percent) was considerably smaller than his lead in the first round in 1974. Moreover, Giscard was strongly challenged by the neo-Gaullist leader, Jacques Chirac, who received 18 percent of the votes and refused to commit his party, the RPR, to support Giscard on the second round, although promising to vote for Giscard himself. The fact that the vote for Communist party leader Georges Marchais dropped to 15 percent also worked rather paradoxically in favor of Mitterrand, since there was reassurance to anti-Communist voters that a vote for Mitterrand would not imply Communist dominance within his government. On the second round of voting on May 10 Mitterrand's victory by a margin of 51.7 to 48.3 percent was thus due to a combination of factors including the poor state of the economy, Giscard's personal unpopularity, party infighting on the right, Mitterrand's calm campaign, and a general desire for change. Yet even this shift, which produced what most commentators regarded as a stunning victory, gave Mitterrand a margin in the popular vote of only 1,066,811 out of a total vote of 30,362,385. Moreover the sharp social cleavage represented by the vote was dramatically portrayed the day after the election when the stock market was compelled to suspend trading because of frantic selling pressure, and the franc collapsed to 5.5 to the dollar (compared to 4.4 six months earlier). Even more graphic were the crowds that swarmed into the streets of Paris to celebrate the first victory of a leftist party since the death of the Fourth Republic.

In the June 1981 parliamentary elections that followed Mitterrand's dissolution of the National Assembly, the French electorate gave him a much stronger mandate to carry through his program of reforms. In the first round of balloting, the Socialist party received 37.5 percent of the vote, while the Gaullists (RPR) received only 20.8 percent, and the UDF (the party of defeated President Giscard d'Estaing) polled 19.2 percent. Although the Communists improved their performance slightly in comparison with the presidential election, they still received only 16.2 percent. On the second round of balloting, the swing to the Socialists became a landslide, leaving them with an absolute majority — 269 seats out of the 491 in the Assembly. All of the other parties had suffered disaster. The Communists had fallen from 86 seats in the previous Assembly to 44, the RPR from 155 to 83, and the UDF from 119 to 61. Mitterrand, moreover, by careful supervision of the choice of candidates of his party, had ensured that at least half of the Socialists elected were so-called *Mitterrandistes*, supporters of his own version of reforms to be implemented.

The new government he selected after the elections reflected his determination to press ahead rapidly to fulfill his election pledges. His premier, Pierre Mauroy, was a person of working-class background, a long-time Socialist, and mayor of Lille, the capital of one of France's most industrialized departments. To carry through one of his central pledges – the decentralization of France's administrative structure – he chose veteran Socialist Gaston Defferre who as mayor of Marseilles was personally acquainted with the grievances of the south and of Corsica. The decline in Communist strength, which emphasized their junior role in the Socialist-Communist partnership, made it possible for Mitterrand to offer them only four cabinet positions (Transport, Public Administration, Health, Professional Training). He also brought several women into his government, the most significant appointment being the choice of Edith Cresson as Minister of Agriculture.

Within weeks, the reform program was well under way. The death penalty was abolished. An amnesty released thousands of prisoners from jail. The State Security Court, which had been used to try political offenders ranging from terrorists favoring a French Algeria to Breton nationalists, was abolished. Economic promises were also given early priority. The minimum wage was raised by 10 percent, and allowances for the handicapped and aged were increased by 25 percent. The work week was to be shortened to 35 hours by 1985. An attack was mounted on unemployment by grant of large credits to small and medium-sized businesses for creation of jobs, while the government itself was to offer work to over 200,000 people. Part of these costs were to be paid by surtaxes levied on exceptionally high salaries and on expense accounts. Perhaps more important in the long run, the government announced that it would begin to redistribute not only the income but the wealth of the French people, by increasing inheritance taxes and by imposing a new levy of between 0.5 and 2 percent on the total wealth of those whose possessions exceeded 3 million francs in value.

The decentralization program was pushed through the Assembly in July in a dramatic session intended to reverse three centuries of increasing concentration of power in Paris. The prefect in each department, traditionally the all-powerful representative of the Paris government, was to be renamed commissar of the republic; they would lose direct authority over the department, but remain as the state's representatives for such services as police, finances, and the military forces. Power was to devolve on regional councils, who were to be elected by universal suffrage and given direct control over a greatly increased share of local expenditure. In September 1981, legislation was introduced in parliament for the nationalization of most of the remaining private banks and of eleven industrial companies in such fields as aircraft production, steel, chemicals, and electronics.

The extent to which Mitterrand and the Socialist majority in the Assembly can alleviate France's deep-rooted problems is uncertain, and the French economic and political situation remains extremely volatile.[11] Regional minority problems remain, in spite of considerable economic progress, and may occasionally erupt into violence. Such violence seems likely to provoke disenchantment among the minority groups themselves, however, and the state is capable of keeping the disorder under control. Large parts of the country will continue to feel themselves disadvantaged and perhaps exploited in comparison with the north, the east, and especially the Paris region, but the continuance of large-scale government programs for the benefit of the less developed regions and the decentralization of administration will probably show greater results in the coming decade than they have previously, simply because an infrastructure had to be created before an economic takeoff in those areas could become feasible. The contrast in wealth, income, and economic opportunity of the different groups of French society remains a more threatening problem. The election of Mitterrand was a mandate for change. But since the reforms proposed involve transformation of the most deep-rooted institutions of French society, attempts to implement such a program will inevitably produce new confrontations, even if it is a different half of the population that feels aggrieved.

9

The United States and France in the 1980s

Of all the Western allies, France has been the most troublesome for American policymakers—and perhaps the most irritating to the American public. It is hard to have one's policies opposed with what appears at times to be almost deliberate provocation. It is annoying to be portrayed to the world as an imperialist power seeking both economic and political hegemony. It is irritating to have one's culture and way of life demeaned. Undoubtedly all these things have happened and will go on happening. Yet the essential conclusion of this book is that the relationship between France and the United States is basically healthy, in spite of passing indispositions. Both countries need the relationship, and both should (and probably will) attempt to improve it.

The political objectives of any government in France—Gaullist, Giscardien, or Socialist (though obviously not Communist)—are likely to be in rough harmony with those of the United States. The constant reaffirmation of the values that the two countries have shared since the American revolution (and that form the staple of public addresses during state visits by the presidents of the two countries) are more than empty rhetoric. Public opinion polls in France, although they may show that the United States is regarded as imperialist, show that the French also have felt the United States to be one of their most reliable friends. Even the Americanization of many of the superficial features of French life, from the snack bar to popular slang, is proof of French fascination with the modernity represented by the United States. The attitude of the French elite, which snapped up 400,000 copies of Jean-Jacques Servan-Schreiber's book, *The American Challenge*, in 1967—the best sales record for that period in French publishing history—was itself a sign of French recognition of the value of learning from the United States. Paradoxically, in the past decade the French perception of the decline in the economic and military position of the United States vis-à-vis the Soviet Union has been a reminder of their own fragile position in a world confrontation and of their dependence for their own continuing autonomy upon the defense capacity of the United States. It may not be fanciful to suggest that where belief in American weakness may have pushed the West Germans toward greater independence in the past decade, the same belief may have made the French less jealous of their own freedom of action, or at the very least may have made them less fearful of coordinating their actions with those of the United States.

During the presidency of François Mitterrand there will obviously be considerable differences of emphasis in French policy from that of Giscard d'Estaing. But there is no doubt that the new regime, as was argued in Chapter 1, will continue to work toward a bettering of relations within the Western alliance in the broadest sense, even if there is dispute over specific issues. Given this general alignment of goals between the French and American governments, it is possible to make a number of specific policy recommendations for the mutually beneficial improvement of relations in the future.

I. *Economic Policy*

a. Trade relations between the United States and France should be considerably increased. In addition to the more traditional exports of luxury goods, food, and wine, the United States should welcome increased imports of heavy and light engineering products from France.

Attempts to restrict importation of automobiles or tires from France would be counterproductive, not only by creating a protectionist attitude but also by inviting reprisals against American exports to France of goods of high technology and possibly also of agricultural goods. In the future the United States cannot, however, expect to run the continually favorable balance of trade with France that it has since the Second World War. France will have increasing difficulty covering a deficit of over one billion dollars in trade with the United States by exports to other industrial countries.

b. The United States should draw more upon French expertise in such areas as hotel construction and administration and in provision of mass transportation systems.

c. French capital should be encouraged to invest in the United States, following the example of the initial investments of such companies as Renault.

d. The activity of American international corporations in France should be less concentrated, and great efforts should be made to avoid perpetuating the kind of monopoly situation existing in business machines and information processing that has in the past produced a French backlash against those companies.

e. French efforts to reduce their balance-of-payments deficits by opening up new avenues of trade with the oil-exporting countries should be encouraged, especially as the diversification of economic ties between the Moslem world and the West helps create a politically beneficial network of interest.

f. The present virtually unrestricted competition between the United States and France for sales of arms to the Third World countries should be replaced by a more coordinated policy in which both economic and political criteria are studied jointly by the two countries before massive arms sales are negotiated.

g. Strengthening of the American dollar and control of inflation in the United States will in the long run benefit France as well as the United States, by reducing the present chaos of the international monetary situation as well as reducing the temptation of the oil-exporting countries constantly to increase their prices.

II. *Military Policy*

a. Coordination of French military planning with that of the NATO powers should be encouraged. A specific role for France in the defense of West Germany must be negotiated. Long-term concepts on the development of the nuclear forces of France and the United States should be harmonized.

b. It should be recognized that French possession of a credible nuclear force gives Western Europe the assurance that it will not be relegated to the role of a nuclear battlefield between the two superpowers, and at the same time, it reduces the temptation for France to seek its own or even a Western European neutralization.

c. France should be encouraged to continue to assume, and in certain cases to increase, its international strategic role. French naval and air power has been increasingly used to monitor the Soviet naval presence in the Mediterranean, and the French have assigned themselves an important role, through their bases in Djibouti and Mayotte, in policing the Indian Ocean.

d. French military intervention in Africa has probably been, *in toto*, beneficial in preventing the destabilization of the French-speaking African states, and it is to be expected that France will continue to maintain an active role in Africa. However, greater cooperation—if only by prior consultation—with the United States and its other allies might be invaluable in preventing France from making such errors as the maintenance in power of Bokassa in the Central African Republic and in leaving the way open in Chad for the entry of Libya.

III. *Policy Toward the Third World and Communist Countries*

a. France's preeminent role in maintaining relationships between the West and the French-speaking states of Africa, including Zaïre, should continue. During the Mitterrand presidency, it is to be expected that France's role will be conceived more as the provider of economic aid than as a political regulator using military intervention. France should, however, be encouraged to maintain its forces in those areas where the economic security of the West is involved, such as in the uranium deposits in Niger.

b. France should maintain its multiplicity of contacts with the Arab world. Diversity of suppliers, even for the most radical countries, enables them to maintain their independence of the blocs and thereby lessens the danger of conflict in the Middle East being escalated into a confrontation of the superpowers. France should be aided, if necessary, in its determination to prevent the destabilization and possible over-throw of such middle-of-the-road governments as that of Tunisia.

c. The United States should encourage France to seek an orderly transition of power in its overseas departments and territories. The growing violence of the independence movements in Guadeloupe and Martinique is fed by worsening ethnic relations and leaves the way open for eventual takeover by extremist forces.

d. It is unlikely that France's relations with the Communist countries will improve during the Mitterrand presidency, but no Western interest would be served by an interruption of the many-sided relationships that de Gaulle, Pompidou, and Giscard d'Estaing labored to open with the Soviet Union and other Communist countries. However, coordination of American and French economic policy toward the Communist bloc would be of considerable value, especially where massive loans to coun-tries like Poland involve the stability of the Western financial system. France should also be welcomed into such potentially fruitful negotia-tions as the MBFR talks and perhaps into any future SALT discussions.

IV. *West European Policy*

a. It is essential that France again take up the cause of European polit-ical integration. The European Community, restricted to economic tasks and denied its political vocation primarily as a result of Gaullist pressure, is in great danger at this time because the public in the Com-munity sees no political progress to offset the economic decline. The French should again take the lead in increasing the powers of the Com-mission and the European Parliament.

b. A close Franco-German partnership remains essential to the stabil-ity of Western Europe. The election of a Socialist president in France in 1981 and the reelection of a Socialist chancellor in West Germany in 1980 promises broadening of the relationship to include closer contacts of the working classes of the two countries and thus revives the partner-ship as it was originally conceived in the early 1960s.

V. *France's Internal Policy*

Although direct attempts to influence the revolution of France's inter-nal policy can only be counterproductive, the United States remains vitally interested in the capacity of France to correct its own internal divisions. Hence the United States can only favor efforts by the French government to correct (a) grievances of ethnic and regional minorities, (b) regional economic imbalance, (c) inequitable distribution of wealth and of income, and (d) domination of government and the professions by entrenched elites. Such long-term programs of reform, many of which have already been undertaken, are essential for the social stability of France and hence for its capacity to exercise the world role that it seeks and the United States should welcome.

Notes

INTRODUCTION

1. Institut National de la Statistique et des Etudes Economiques, *Annuaire statistique de la France, 1979* (Paris: INSEE, 1979), p. 55*.

2. Ibid.

3. *L'Express*, December 24, 1979, p. 28.

CHAPTER ONE

1. Charles de Gaulle, *The War Memoirs of Charles de Gaulle. Unity, 1942–1944*, trans. Richard Howard (New York: Simon and Schuster, 1959), p. 88.

2. Alfred Grosser, *Les Occidentaux. Les Pays d'Europe et les Etats-Unis depuis la guerre* (Paris: Fayard, 1978), p. 172. Grosser's book is indispensable for an understanding of American relations with Europe, and particularly with France, since 1945. It has been translated into English as *The Western Alliance: European American Relations since 1945* (New York: Continuum, 1980).

3. The "inspirer" of both the ECSC and the Common Market was Jean Monnet, the former head of the French Planning Commissariat and the

Frenchman most influential in the decision-making circles of both politics and economics in the United States. Monnet's close friends in the United States included Eisenhower, Dulles, Acheson, George Ball, and John McCloy. Grosser, *Les Occidentaux*, pp. 135–41.

4. Charles de Gaulle, *Mémoires d'espoir. Le Renouveau 1958–1962* (Paris: Plon, 1970), p. 222.

5. Ibid., p. 176.

6. Ibid., p. 175.

7. F. Roy Willis, *France, Germany, and the New Europe, 1945–1967* (rev. ed.: Stanford: Stanford University Press, 1968), pp. 297–98, 302–304.

8. Television interview, December 14, 1965.

9. Marc Ullman, "Security Aspects in French Foreign Policy," *Atlantic Community Quarterly*, vol. 12, no. 1 (Spring 1974), p. 17.

10. Marie Claude Smouts, "French Foreign Policy: The Domestic Debate," *International Affairs*, vol. 53, no. 1 (January 1977), pp. 38–39.

11. Dorothy Pickles, "The Decline of Gaullist Foreign Policy," *International Affairs*, vol. 51, no. 2 (April 1975), p. 227.

12. *L'Express*, May 17, 1980, p. 46.

13. Ibid., p. 72.

14. Ibid., March 12, 1982, p. 43.

CHAPTER TWO

1. De Gaulle, *Mémoires d'espoir*, p. 139.

2. Jean Fourastié, *Les Trente glorieuses ou la révolution invisible de 1946 à 1975* (Paris: Fayard, 1979).

3. INSEE, *Annuaire statistique, 1979*, p. 55*.

4. Fourastié, *Les Trente glorieuses*, p. 260.

5. Ibid., pp. 36, 46, 47.

6. Gordon Wright, *Rural Revolution in France. The Peasantry in the Twentieth Century* (Stanford: Stanford University Press, 1964), p. 145.

7. Ministère de l'Economie, *Le Budget économique de la France pour 1980* (Paris: Ministère de l'Economie, 1980), n.p.

8. INSEE, *Annuaire statistique, 1977*, p. 221.

9. *L'Express*, January 26, 1980, p. 33.

10. INSEE, *Statistiques et indicateurs des régions françaises, 1978* (Paris: INSEE, 1979), p. 263.

11. Fourastié, *Les Trente glorieuses*, p. 138.

12. Ibid., p. 36.

13. INSEE, *Tableaux de l'économie française, 1979* (Paris: INSEE, 1979), p. 49.

14. Ibid., p. 151.

15. Ibid., pp. 98–99.

16. *L'Express*, February 23, 1980, pp. 39–43.

17. INSEE, *Tableaux de l'économie française, 1979*, p. 96.

18. Grosser, *Les Occidentaux*, p. 284. The inability of the French government to protect a high technology industry like electronics in the face of intense competition in the international marketplace is discussed in John Zysman, *Political Strategies for Industrial Order: State, Market, and Industry in France* (Berkeley, Los Angeles: University of California Press, 1977), especially pp. 139–55.

19. Grosser, *Les Occidentaux*, p. 381.

20. *L'Express*, January 19, 1980, p. 51.

21. *Financial Times* (London), January 31, 1980.

22. *Le Monde*, May 22, 1979.

23. United States Arms Control and Disarmament Agency, *World Military Expenditures and Arms Transfers 1968-1977* (Washington, D.C.: USACDA, 1979), pp. 155–57.

24. United States Department of Defense, *Foreign Military Sales and Military Assistance Facts, December 1979* (Washington, D.C.: U.S. Government Printing Office, 1979), p. 17.

25. See the valuable article by Edward A. Kolodziej, "France and the Arms Trade," *International Affairs*, vol. 56, no. 1 (January 1980), pp. 54–72.

26. Stockholm International Peace Research Institute (SIPRI), *Arms Trade Registers. The Arms Trade with the Third World* (Cambridge, Mass., and London, England: The MIT Press, 1975), p. 68.

27. Ibid., p. 62.

28. *L'Express*, January 26, 1980, p. 35.

29. Anthony Sampson, *The Arms Bazaar. From Lebanon to Lockheed* (New York: Viking, 1977), pp. 260–76.

CHAPTER THREE

1. INSEE, *Tableaux de l'économie française, 1979*, pp. 151, 153. The military expenditures of the Soviet Union in 1977 were estimated to be 13.3 percent of the national income, according to the United States Arms Control and Disarmament Agency; between 11 and 13, percent, according to the London International Institute for Strategic Studies (IISS); and 8 percent, according to

the Stockholm International Peace Research Institute. See USACDA, *World Military Expenditures and Arms Transfers, 1968–1977*, p. 61; International Institute for Strategic Studies, *The Military Balance, 1978–1979* (London: International Institute for Strategic Studies, 1978), p. 88; and Stockholm International Peace Research Institute, *World Armaments and Disarmament. SIPRI Yearbook 1979* (London: Taylor and Francis, 1979), p. 39. The French statistical office INSEE accepts the figures of the IISS.

2. Lothar Ruehl, *La Politique militaire de la Ve république* (Paris: Presses de la Fondation Nationale des Sciences Politiques, 1976), pp. 338–40, 345; Raoul Girardet, *Problèmes contemporains de défense nationale* (Paris: Dalloz, 1974), pp. 167–69.

3. John Keegan *et al.*, *World Armies* (London: Macmillan, 1979), pp. 222, 225.

4. Ruehl, *Politique militaire*, p. 295.

5. Ibid., p. 338.

6. International Institute for Strategic Studies, *Military Balance, 1978–1979*, pp. 22–24; Keegan, *World Armies*, p. 221.

7. Colonel Arnaud P. Loubens and Captain M. Valentin, "The French Armored Division," *Armor* (September–October 1980), pp. 22–25.

8. Stockholm International Peace Research Institute, *Yearbook, 1979*, pp. 358, 361.

9. On the development of the French bomb, see General Charles Ailleret, *L'Aventure atomique française. Comment naquit la force de frappe* (Paris: Bernard Grasset, 1968).

10. Ruehl, *Politique militaire*, pp. 228, 256, 281, 305–306.

11. Curiously enough, it has been argued in France that the fact that the Plateau d'Albion missiles can only be destroyed by a massive deployment of Soviet nuclear striking power makes them more effective as a dissuasion than the nuclear submarines that, though elusive, can be destroyed with a minor use of force by an aggressor who can remain incognito. See Ivan Margine, "L'Avenir de la dissuasion," *Défense Nationale* (April 1978), pp. 11–13. The modernization of the nuclear forces is described in Paul Stares, "The Future of the French Strategic Force," *International Security Review*, vol. V, no. 2 (Summer 1980), pp. 231–57 and in Jean Klein, "France's Military Policy in the 1980s," *International Security Review*, vol. V, no. 4 (Winter 1980–1981), pp. 455–76.

12. De Gaulle, *Mémoirs d'espoir*, p. 213.

13. Jean Klein, "Continuité et ouverture dans la politique française en matière de désarmement," *Politique Etrangère*, vol. 44, no. 2 (1979), pp. 213–14.

14. Jean Klein, "La France, l'arme nucléaire et la défense de l'Europe," *Politique Etrangère*, vol. 44, no. 3 (1979), p. 464.

15. Ibid., p. 477.

CHAPTER FOUR

1. The Syrian and Lebanese governments feared that General de Gaulle was sending additional troops to their countries as a means of pressure to gain greater privileges for France in the negotiations on future relations following independence. See Jean Baptiste Duroselle, *Histoire diplomatique de 1919 à nos jours* (3rd ed.; Paris: Dalloz, 1962), pp. 488–91.

2. Guy de Carmoy, *Les Politiques étrangères de la France, 1944–1966* (Paris: Table Ronde, 1967), pp. 216–17.

3. Pierre Vidal-Naquet, *La Raison d'état* (Paris: Les Editions de Minuit, 1962), pp. 20, 25, cited in W. W. Kulski, *De Gaulle and the World. The Foreign Policy of the Fifth French Republic* (Syracuse: Syracuse University Press, 1966), p. 329.

4. Ibid., p. 321, citing a poll taken by *Jeune Afrique* in 1965. The second most popular person was marathon runner Abébé Bikila.

5. The immediate effect of de Gaulle's action was to thrust Guinea into closer dependence upon the Soviet Union and the East European Communist countries during the two years (1959–1961) of desperate economic troubles. It received from them some food and manufactured goods, large quantities of trucks and tractors, and engineers and other technical specialists. But by 1961, with the economy declining still further, Touré sought and received American aid, which reached $16 million in 1962 alone; and in 1963 he patched up his quarrel with France. But, in 1965, the pendulum swung again. Touré quarreled with the French and revived his relations not only with Russia but also with China. See Guy de Lusignan, *French-Speaking Africa Since Independence* (London: Pall Mall Press, 1969), pp. 180–98, and Roland Vezeau, *L'Afrique face au communisme* (Paris: Edimpra, 1967), pp. 59–62.

6. The Constitution of the Fifth Republic, in Part XII, replaced the French Union (which had itself replaced the French colonial empire in the Constitution of the Fourth Republic in 1946), with a French Community in which the new African states would be self-governing internally. When the African states opted for independence in 1960, the brief-lived Community fell apart, and most of its organs were abolished. Behind the facade of continuing collaboration was the reality of a growing ideological division of the French-speaking African states. Two (Guinea and Mali) were radical in goal, and leaning toward the Communist bloc. Six chose to remain closely tied to France (Senegal, Madagas-

car, Gabon, Chad, the Central African Republic, and Congo-Brazzaville). The remainder sought a middle-of-the-road position.

7. On the agreements, see Pierre Lellouche and Dominique Moisi, "French Policy in Africa: A Lonely Struggle against Destabilization," *International Security*, no. 3:4 (Spring, 1979), pp. 111–14. The agreements gave France a privileged, and in some cases virtually exclusive, access to strategic raw materials, including oil, gas, uranium, helium, and beryllium.

8. "Le Tiers monde et nous," *Cahiers Français*, no. 167 (new ed., February 1977), p. 51.

9. Lellouche and Moisi, "French Policy in Africa," pp. 114, 116.

10. *Cahiers Français*, no. 167, p. 44.

11. *Le Monde*, February 28, 1964; cited in Lellouche and Moisi, "French Policy in Africa," p. 117. Waldemar A. Nielsen notes that one reason for the large number of French interventions was "to help create a 'climate of order' in the face of an epidemic of coups in French Africa engineered by the new armies France had helped create, equip, and train." See his *The Great Powers and Africa* (New York: Praeger, 1969), p. 119. The most memorable examples of coups by these newly created armies were the overthrow and assassination of President Sylvanis Olympio of Togo, which the French chose to permit; the overthrow of President Fulbert Youlou in Congo-Brazzaville in August 1963 after he refused French aid; and the ouster of President Hubert Maga in Dahomey in October 1963. For a discussion of military coups and the regimes they installed in Dahomey, Togo, and Congo-Brazzaville, see Samuel Decalo, *Coups and Army Rule in Africa: Studies in Military Style* (New Haven and London: Yale University Press, 1976), especially pp. 52–53, 139–40, and pp. 97–99. On the foiled coups in Niger and Gabon, see De Lusignan, *French-Speaking Africa*, pp. 157–59, 103–107. Diori was finally ousted in April 1974. M'ba died in 1967.

12. The Madagascar government renegotiated its defense agreements with France in 1973, and compelled the French to close their base at Diego Suarez. France redeployed its land and naval forces to the islands of Réunion and Mayotte (in the Comores) and to five support points on other Indian Ocean islands (Juan de Nova, Europa, Bassas de India, Tromelin, and the Glorious Islands). Lellouche and Moisi, "French Policy in Africa," p. 116, footnote 17.

13. See De Lusignan, *French-Speaking Africa*, pp. 113–14, 121.

14. Cited Nielsen, *The Great Powers and Africa*, p. 120.

15. Lellouche and Moisi, "French Policy in Africa," p. 118.

16. See the testimony of Sean Gervasi to the U.S. Congress, House, Committee on International Relations, Subcommittee on Africa, July 1977, cited in L. H. Gann and Peter Duignan, *South Africa: War, Revolution, or Peace?* (Stan-

ford: Hoover Institution Press, 1978), pp. 28–29; Stockholm International Peace Research Institute, *Arms Trade Registers*, pp. 93–95.

17. See the essays by Colin Legum and David E. Albright, in David E. Albright, ed., *Communism in Africa* (Bloomington and London: Indiana University Press, 1980), especially pp. 26, 38–40. On Soviet penetration in Africa after 1975, see Ian Greig, *The Communist Challenge to Africa: An Analysis of Contemporary Soviet, Chinese, and Cuban Policies* (Richmond, England: Foreign Affairs Publishing Co., 1977).

18. General Méry, "L'Avenir de nos armées," *Défense nationale* (June 1978), pp. 20–21.

19. *L'Express*, December 22, 1979, pp. 34–38, noted that France's African policy was made in secret by the president with the aid of three long-time experts on Africa: Minister of Cooperation Robert Gally, Guy Georgy, the director of African affairs at the foreign ministry, and René Journiac at the Elysée palace. Their personal acquaintance with African personalities and their ability to act in secrecy in the use of military power explain France's ability to intervene so rapidly in African affairs. Guy Georgy describes the new policy in "Les Nouveaux aspects de la politique africaine," *Projet*, no. 141 (January 1980), pp. 57–63. Journiac was killed in the crash of a small plane in Cameroon in February 1980.

20. Greig, *The Communist Challenge to Africa*, p. 29; Lellouche and Moisi, "French Policy in Africa," p. 122, footnote 35.

21. Ibid., p. 124.

22. On events in Chad through 1967, see De Lusignan, *French-Speaking Africa*, pp. 114–21. On the events since 1967, see "Le Tchad, maintenant," *Projet* (June 1979), pp. 748–54; Michel Montenay, "Tchad: les trois erreurs de Giscard," *Le Matin*, March 30, 1979; Agnes Thivent, "L'Impossible mission de l'armée française," *Le Monde Diplomatique* (March 1980).

23. *L'Express*, April 19, 1980.

24. *Le Figaro*, May 19, 1980.

25. *Le Monde*, July 21, 1978, cited Lellouche and Moisi, "French Policy in Africa," p. 52. Translation modified.

26. *L'Express*, December 22, 1979, p. 38.

27. Henri Raison, "Y a-t-il *une politique* africaine de la France?" *Projet*, no. 141 (June 1979), pp. 65–66. Raison notes that recently the French ambassador in Gabon gave up his post to become president of a uranium mines company.

28. *Le Monde*, June 16, 1978, cited in Lellouche and Moisi, "French Policy in Africa," p. 131.

29. *L'Express*, December 22, 1979, p. 38.

CHAPTER FIVE

1. Cited in Tony Smith, *The French Stake in Algeria, 1945–1962* (Ithaca, N.Y.: Cornell University Press, 1978), p. 27.

2. William B. Cohen, "Legacy of Empire: The Algerian Connection," *Journal of Contemporary History*, vol. 15, no. 1 (January 1980), p. 113–14. Cohen notes that with two million followers the Moslem faith was the second largest in France. There were 750,000 Protestants, and 500,000 Jews, of whom 200,000 had come from the Maghreb in the 1950s and 1960s.

3. Cited in Edward A. Kolodziej, *French International Policy under De Gaulle and Pompidou: The Politics of Grandeur* (Ithaca, N.Y.: Cornell University Press, 1974), p. 464.

4. Cited in Paul Balta and Claudine Rulleau, *La Politique arabe de la France de De Gaulle à Pompidou* (Paris: Sinbad, 1973), p. 60.

5. Kolodziej, *French International Policy*, p. 536.

6. Cohen, "Legacy of Empire," pp. 110–15.

7. Stockholm International Peace Research Institute, *Arms Trade Registers*, pp. 66–67.

8. Cited in Daniel Colard, "La Politique méditerranéenne et proche-orientale de G. Pompidou," *Politique Etrangère*, no. 3 (1978), p. 304.

9. Kolodziej argues that the moderate, pro-American attitude of Tunisian President Bourguiba, as well as his personal disharmony with de Gaulle, made the French unwilling to appear closely aligned with Tunisia. "The moderate nature of the Tunisian and Moroccan regimes...did not fit the desired image of a progressive France willing to cooperate with any regime, however revolutionary or Marxist." Kolodziej, *French International Policy*, pp. 484–85.

10. Stockholm International Peace Research Institute, *Yearbook, 1979*, pp. 224–26; International Institute for Strategic Studies, *The Military Balance, 1978–1979*, p. 40. The arms deal with the Soviet Union was concluded during the visit to Tunisia of Soviet Premier Aleksei N. Kosygin in May 1975.

11. *L'Express*, February 9, 1980, pp. 52–53; Ibid., February 16, 1980, pp. 47–49.

12. André Fontaine, "Le Proche-Orient d'hier à demain," *Politique Etrangère*, no. 1, vol. 45 (March 1980), p. 164.

13. For a pro-Israeli discussion of his meaning, see Claude Clément, *Israel et la Ve République* (Paris: Oliver Orban, 1978), pp. 122–25. The French position is explained in Paul Balta, "La France et le monde arabe: II–Les réalités politiques," *Revue de Défense Nationale*, vol. XXVI (June 1970), pp. 924–34. Pompidou was especially outraged in December 1969 when the Israelis, with the connivance of the Délégation Ministérielle pour l'Armement, were able to

sail out of Cherbourg harbor five torpedo boats whose delivery was banned by the embargo.

14. The fluctuations of Soviet influence in Iraq are described in Hélène Carrère d'Encausse, *La Politique soviétique au moyen-orient 1955–1975* (Paris: Presses de la Fondation Nationale des Sciences Politiques, 1975), pp. 125–34, 231–44, 294–295.

15. Philippe Rondot, "L'Irak d'aujourd'hui, de la fermeté au réalisme," *Politique Etrangère*, no. 3, vol. 43 (1978), pp. 311–15; Stockholm International Peace Research Institute, *Yearbook, 1979*, pp. 218–19.

16. *L'Express*, July 19, 1980, pp. 58–59; October 25, 1980, p. 47. The magazine claimed to have certain knowledge that Israel had sent two Phantom jets across the south of Syria to hit the nuclear reactor.

CHAPTER SIX

1. Cited Grosser, *Les Occidentaux*, p. 272.

2. Documentation Française, *La Politique étrangère de la France: Textes et documents*, 2e semestre, 1974, p. 232.

3. Ibid.

4. *Le Figaro*, May 24–25, 1980; *Le Monde*, May 25–26, 1980.

5. *Le Figaro*, October 28, 1975; *L'Express*, May 31, 1980, p. 40.

6. Cited W. W. Kulski, *De Gaulle and the World: The Foreign Policy of the Fifth Republic* (Syracuse: Syracuse University Press, 1966), p. 301.

7. Kolodziej, *French International Policy*, pp. 364–75.

8. Message to the National Assembly on December 11, 1962, cited in Alfred Grosser, "General de Gaulle and the Foreign Policy of the Fifth Republic," *International Affairs*, vol. 39, no. 2 (April 1963), p. 207.

9. Cited Kolodziej, *French International Policy*, p. 352.

10. *L'Express*, May 17, 1980, p. 42.

11. See his speeches reported in France, Ministère des Affairs Etrangères, *Les Relations franco-soviétiques: Textes et documents, 1965–1976* (Paris: Documentation Française, 1976), p. 157. He was still aggrieved in November, when interviewed about his trip to the Soviet Union, about the general tendency to regard détente as the appanage of the three great powers—Russia, America, and China. See *L'Annee politique, 1975*, p. 167.

12. Poll conducted by the Institute Public SA, for *Quotidien de Paris*, June 3, 1980. Asked at the same time which leaders displayed the greatest firmness toward Russia (rated on a scale of 1 to 6), the French people polled felt that the

weakest were the three French leaders. Socialist François Mitterrand received only 3.2; Gaullist Jacques Chirac 3.6; and Giscard d'Estaing 3.9. Jimmy Carter received 4.4, Ronald Reagan 4.6. At the head of the list was British Prime Minister Margaret Thatcher with 5.1.

13. Pisani, *La France dans le conflit économique mondial*, p. 56. It required five years of negotiation before the Soviet Union gave the LMT company a contract to build a factory capable of producing one million telephone cables a year.

14. *Le Monde*, May 18–19, 1980.

15. News release from *Izvestia*, Novosti Press Agency, March 24, 1976.

16. *The Economist* (London), May 5, 1979. The principal protocols through 1975 are reprinted in *Les Relations franco-soviétiques*, pp. 7–8, 18–22, 83–84, 105–106, 168–73. The more recent protocols are published in *Le Monde*, June 23, 1977, and April 29–30, 1979.

17. Kolodziej, *French International Policy*, p. 369.

18. Ibid., p. 375.

19. *Les Relations franco-soviétiques*, p. 91.

20. *L'Année politique, 1975*, p. 142. During the ambitious visit of June 17–20, 1975, Giscard visited Warsaw, Katowice, and Auschwitz. He returned to Poland in October 1976 and September 1978, and received Gierek in France in September 1977 and September 1979. The close relations thus established permitted Giscard to use the excuse of an invitation from Gierek to meet with Brezhnev in Warsaw in 1980.

21. *L'Express*, September 27, 1980, pp. 42–46.

CHAPTER SEVEN

1. Cited *Projet*, no. 141 (January 1980), p. 24. Speech in Brest, 1960.

2. In 1976, Giscard d'Estaing could still remark, at a time when the French were disturbed at what seemed to be a revival of neo-Nazism in Germany: "I consider that it is important for the military balance of our continent that the French army should be of the same order of size as the other army of our continent, that is to say the German army." *L'Année politique, 1976*, pp. 198–99. As Alfred Grosser has remarked, the French believe that the ideal size for a German army is one larger than the Soviet but smaller than the French. On the ongoing tension in the 1970s, see Alfred Frisch, "Les relations franco-allemandes: Une amitié solide et fragile à la fois," *Documents: Revue des Questions Allemandes* (September 1976), pp. 5–17.

3. De Gaulle, *Mémoires de guerre*, III, pp. 222, 179–80.

4. Two good surveys of the early efforts at reconciliation are Gilbert Ziebura, *Die deutsch-französischen Beziehungen seit 1945: Mythen und Realitäten* (Pfullingen: Neske, 1970) and Raymond Poidevin and Jacques Bariéty, *Les Relations franco-allemandes, 1815–1975* (Paris: Armand Colin, 1977), pp. 325–42.

5. Text of the treaty in *Le Monde*, January 24, 1963. English translation issued by Ambassade de France, Washington, D.C., *French Affairs*, no. 152.

6. *Le Monde*, July 3, 1963.

7. Gérard Valin, "La France et l'Allemagne de l'Ouest face à la crise de l'énergie," *Allemagnes d'Aujourd'hui* (September–October, 1974), pp. 31–43.

8. *L'Express*, July 12, 1980, p. 52.

9. *Le Point*, February 11, 1980, p. 36.

10. French observers tend to regard the West German need to keep open the human exchanges with East Germany as a guarantee that no German government could follow the American in abandoning détente. See the editorial of Oliver Chevrillon in *Le Point*, February 11, 1980. "If the Atlantic alliance were to collapse, Germany would not change from one camp to another, it is clear. But it would slide toward neutrality, tipping over Europe by its weight. For the Soviet Union, that victory would be worth several Afghanistans."

11. *Le Nouvel Observateur*, February 11, 1980.

12. Poidevin and Bariéty, *Relations franco-allemandes*, pp. 344–45; INSEE, *Annuaire statistique, 1979*, p. 619.

13. *The Economist*, May 26, 1979.

14. According to Pompidou in 1971, "The truth is that there is a conception of Europe and it is a question of knowing if Great Britain's conception is truly European." Cited Kolodziej, *French International Policy*, p. 411. Kolodziej gives a succinct summary of the British negotiations for entry on pp. 405–25.

15. INSEE, *Tableaux de l'économie française, 1979*, p. 139.

16. *Le Monde*, July 13, 1978. To dramatize these views, he visited Madrid in June 1978 and Lisbon in July 1978 and attended the signature in Athens of the agreement on Greek entry into the Community on May 28, 1979.

17. *Le Monde*, May 17, 1979.

18. INSEE, *Tableaux de l'économie française, 1979*, p. 139.

19. At Hoerdt, Giscard omitted both the reference to Hitler and the name of the state secretary!

20. Interview with *Der Spiegel*, January 1, 1979, cited in Pascal Fontaine, "Giscard d'Estaing et la construction de l'Europe," *Projet*, no. 141 (January 1980), p. 30.

21. "Europe is hope," according to Giscard, "hope that France, active and generous, seeing far and thinking large, will be able, in this rejuvenated Europe, to play the role which belongs to its genius and its brilliant history." *Le Monde*, May 17, 1979.

22. *Quotidien de Paris*, June 3, 1980.

23. Jacques Thibau, *La France colonisée* (Paris: Flammarion, 1980).

24. Grosser, *Les Occidentaux*, p. 403. On the Americanization of the French language, see Henri Godard, *L'Aliénation linguistique. Analyse tetraglossique* (Paris: Flammarion, 1976).

25. The correspondent of *Le Monde*, January 26–27, 1978, commented with some amazement, however, that the average American had little interest in French affairs, except for the activity of the French Communist party.

26. Even the most understanding analysts of the French situation have been "severe," as Stanley Hoffmann admits. See his "No Trumps, No Luck, No Will: Gloomy Thoughts on Europe's Plight," in James Chace and Earl C. Ravenal, eds., *Atlantis Lost: U.S.-European Relations after the Cold War* (New York: New York University Press, 1976), especially pp. 11–14.

27. The French Foreign Minister, Jean François-Poncet, gave the commencement address in 1980 at Wesleyan University, where he had been an exchange student.

CHAPTER EIGHT

1. The most exploited and least powerful of the national minorities within France are the 3.4 million immigrants, one-third of whom come from Algeria, Morocco, and Tunisia. They are subject to deep-seated resentment from the French working class population who, as unemployment grew in 1980 and 1981, resorted to violence to pressure the immigrants to return home.

2. *Le Point*, August 11, 1980, pp. 64–66.

3. French Basques have given help and shelter to the Spanish Basque separatists, especially during the Franco period, but they, themselves, have taken little action against the French state. Most French Basques consider that in a united Basque state they would be a poor agricultural minority in comparison with the other Basques, four times more numerous, who live in the industrialized Basque areas of Spain.

4. INSEE published a groundbreaking study of the wealth of individuals in "Le Patrimoine national," *Economie et Statistique*, no. 114 (September 1979). The size of the different socioprofessional categories of the French population is given in Ibid., no. 110 (April 1979), pp. 60–62. INSEE's authors are especially

critical of the exaggeration of the disparities suggested by Robert Lattes, *La Fortune des français* (Paris: J.-C. Lattes, 1977), pp. 64, 67–71.

5. *Economie et statistique*, no. 114 (September 1979), pp. 123, 124.

6. The complete analysis of the income figures for 1974, which was only completed in 1979, is INSEE, *Les Salaires dans l'industrie, le commerce et les services en 1974*, Collections M 76 (Paris: INSEE, 1979), especially pp. 31–34. See also Documentation Française, *Profil économique de la France*, pp. 53–54, 64; INSEE, *Tableaux économiques de la France, 1979*, pp. 72–75.

7. Alain Peyrefitte, *Le Mal français* (Paris: Plon, 1976), pp. 328–29. On the role of the grandes écoles in forming "state-created elites," see Ezra N. Suleiman, *Elites in French Society: The Politics of Survival* (Princeton: Princeton University Press, 1978).

8. An extensive literature has been published in France during the past two decades to prove that its society is blocked (i.e., incapable of reform from within), the best known being Michel Crozier's *La Société bloquée* (Paris: Seuil, 1970).

9. *L'Express*, November 29, 1980, p. 47.

10. See the special issue, "Conflict and Consensus in France," *West European Politics*, vol. 1, no. 3 (October 1978), especially the article by Vincent Wright, "The French General Election of March 1978: 'La Divine Surprise,'" pp. 24–52.

11. *L'Express*, May 29, 1981; June 26, 1981; and September 4, 1981.

Index